BLACK & WHITE

(and a bit in between)

BLACK & WHITE

(and a bit in between)

Timeless Interiors, Dramatic Accents, and Stylish Collections

Celerie Kemble

Clarkson Potter/Publishers

NEW YORK

Copyright © 2011 by Celerie Kemble

Published in the United States by Clarkson Potter/Publishers, an
imprint of the Crown Publishing Group, a division of Random
House, Inc., New York.
www.crownpublishing.com
www.clarksonpotter.com

CLARKSON POTTER is a trademark and POTTER with colophon
is a registered trademark of Random House, Inc.

Library of Congress Cataloging-in-Publication Data
Kemble, Celerie.
  Black & white (and a bit in between) / Celerie Kemble. — 1st ed.
    p. cm.
1. Black in interior decoration. 2. White in interior decoration.
I. Title. II. Title: Black and white (and a bit in between).
  NK2115.5.C6K46 2011
  747'.94—dc23
                    2011017880

ISBN 978-0-307-71598-2

Printed in China

Principal photography by Zach DeSart
A list of additional photograph credits appears on pages 252–253.

Book design by Stephanie Huntwork
Jacket design by Stephanie Huntwork
Jacket photographs: (front; back, above right) Zack DeSart and
(back, below left) Michael Graydon

10   9   8   7   6   5   4   3   2

First Edition

This book is dedicated to those who let me
think out loud . . . most especially my husband, Boykin,
who is usually sitting the closest.

contents

introduction

"If everything isn't black and white, I say
'Why the hell not?'"
—John Wayne

I CAN'T PRETEND I've ever led my life in black and white. Growing up in Palm Beach, Florida—a bougainvillea-fringed playground where sunsets bathe the roofs and treetops in ruby red and tangerine; where the aqua blue of swimming pools glimmers against the bright pinks and yellows of Lilly Pulitzer dresses and Lacoste shirts; and where even the cars are candy-colored—I was surrounded by every hue in the Technicolor paint kit.

When I headed north for high school and college to the more subdued New England landscape, and later, as I began my adult life in Manhattan, my memory's color index traveled with me. In the fifteen years I've worked as an interior decorator in New York, I've functioned as a kind of human kaleidoscope, someone who walks into a house and unfurls a spectrum of color choices. I present a quince-green, indigo, or hibiscus-pink world to clients who want to escape their beige-on-beige, taupe, brown, or cream-and-tan boxes but who lack the vocabulary or can't quite picture the possibilities.

Not long ago, I noticed that with some clients, paring down the color schemes produced dramatic results. I always find my job exciting because designing interiors is a process of starting afresh, taking risks, and giving shape to the imagination. But I hadn't experimented much with the idea of constraint. Of course, I've always worked within the constraints of budget and my clients' tastes, but as far as color selection, I'd drawn from a riotous abundance of options. Overabundance, really. I wanted to find some parameters, and to try out some black and white truths, to see if they would invigorate my work, and my clients' homes.

It may seem as if my life brims with contentment: I am married to the man I love; I am enraptured by my three children; I work in a field that brings me great joy; I adore my coworkers and not so infrequently my cli-

ents. And yet lately, I'd begun to feel like it was time to leave my comfort zone.

I decided to put aside the crutch of the sixty-four-pack of Crayola crayons (and eight neon colors) and try my hand at the unfamiliar territory of black and white. I'll admit, I was afraid that limiting myself this way would limit my creativity, producing spaces that felt too drab, too stark, too old-fashioned, and too joyless. But instead, as I visited the black and white work of my peers, the grand historic and contemporary black and white residences, and the work of great artists in black and white—the decorator Dorothy Draper, the photographer Cecil Beaton, and the filmmaker Preston Sturges, for example—I realized that a simplified palette can unlock a rich world.

Once I started looking, I saw signs of the expressive power of this minimalist color scheme everywhere around me, whether in nature's dramatic chiaroscuro—dark mountains and pale snow, black rocks and whitecaps, the moon and the night sky—or in the arresting accoutrements of our culture that we don't necessarily register day to day, like pianos and chessboards, white shirts and dark suits, books, newspapers, and crossword puzzles. The language of the two colors I'd neglected was speaking to me, and I listened.

In *The Wizard of Oz,* after Dorothy falls asleep in black-and-white Kansas and wakes in the multicolor fairyland of Oz, she exults, "We must be over the rainbow!" In writing this book, I found that same spirit of exultation by traveling in the reverse direction, from profusion to simplicity—away from the rainbow. *Black and White (and a Bit in Between)* invites you to see that this palette can be freeing instead of limiting. Like a black velvet cloth under diamonds or a white sail against a dark sea, those strong shades not only set each other off and intensify the colors and spaces around them, they also heighten the drama.

Investigating how black and white can be used to create inspiring, tasteful, and beautiful spaces has been a fascinating and difficult process for me, and also invigorating and rewarding, both intellectually and artistically. It's led me—and I hope will guide you—in exciting new creative directions. I couldn't take the liberty of foisting my newfound theories on my clients; nor could I throw my family, household, and bank account into an uproar by attempting a massive redo of my own walls and rooms. Instead, my laboratory has been this book: a gathering place for other peoples' excellent designs, a few of my own, and inspiration for experiments to come.

1 COLOR IN PRACTICE
so what is black, and what is white anyway?

"We think that grass is green, that stones are hard, and that snow is cold. But physics assures us that the greenness of grass, the hardness of stones, and the coldness of snow are not the greenness, hardness, and coldness that we know in our own experience, but something very different."

—Albert Einstein, on Bertrand Russell's *Theory of Knowledge*

PRECEDING PAGES

I used a lot of color throughout this town-
house but opted for a palette-cleansing
black and white starting point. The
scheme connects the foyer to the
stairwell that runs through the house.

ABOVE AND OPPOSITE

As a design vocabulary, these two colors
can be used to create vastly different
moods. A pure white dining room is
flawless in its modern simplicity, while
an ornate iron railing climbs past
arched windows and white walls.

BLACK AND WHITE contain an unsuspected variety of shades, and you
can "exploit them" to create original and powerful spaces. Whether you're
determined to wield this duo in moderation or execute it lavishly in every
room of your home, before you get out your paintbrush it's important to
define the terms.

What is black? What is white? We can all conjure hundreds of images
when we hear those two colors named: salt and pepper, the keys of a piano,
the lines of an asphalt crosswalk, birch bark, gondoliers' stripes. But if we
were to look closely at any of those objects, we'd see that the salt's white has a
silvery sheen; the piano keys have a creamy cast; the crosswalk, on closer
inspection, is dark gray; the birch bark is cream-colored, striped with thin
gold-brown lines. In twilight or shadow, all colors lose their sureness; in
intense sunlight, they shift, too. Try to match a white tablecloth with white
dishes and napkins, and you'll see how many shades of pale there turn out
to be.

It's interesting, then, that there's an ongoing debate about whether black
and white even qualify as colors. A scientist would say that black is just the
absence of light, that it's essentially null and empty. Ironic then, that when
you mix paint in art school, you learn that you have to combine all the primary paint colors to make black. At the other extreme, white represents the
presence of all light . . . but think how corruptible that is in practice. It's the
absence of all pigment, since the addition of any extra hue makes it something
else completely. Black and white is an effect, not an absolute; and it's an effect
that you can insinuate into a room with a few well-chosen signature pieces, or
institute wholesale with a more elaborate design scheme.

10 reasons to embrace black and white

1 It's elegant.

A black and white palette has a special and enduring glamour that dresses up any room.

2 It's versatile.

Over the years, you can add new elements to a black and white base. One new pillow, painting, or sculpture can refresh the entire look.

3 It's practical.

The gravitas of the scheme reduces the number of furniture pieces you need to make a room look complete. Also, nearly everything on the market has a black or a white option, which makes the room comparatively easy to furnish. And black hides dirt, while white slipcovers can be bleached.

4 It's inclusive.

Because a black and white scheme is so unfussy and classic, it camouflages inexpensive items well. This is ideal if you intend to invest in finer pieces down the road—or if you need time to work up the finances to splurge. It can absorb and frame new higher-end pieces gradually.

5 It's classic.

Long after your magenta armchair has gone to Goodwill, the cream silk velvet love seat in your black and white boudoir will stay with you—as will your black and white checkerboard floor, your black lacquerware, and your white china.

6 It's playful.

With a black and white palette, you can take design risks and stretch your imagination, mixing and matching eras, objects, scale, passions, and

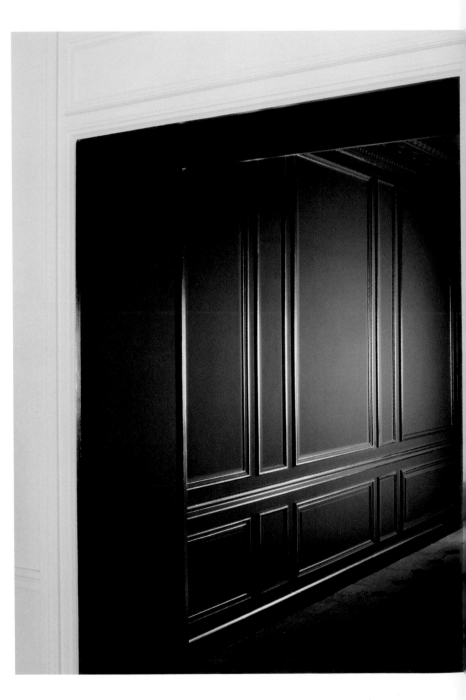

themes—with less chance that your room will end up a mess.

7 It's creative.

Boundaries give you freedom. Shakespeare constrained himself to a limited meter, and in it, wrote the world's greatest plays. By narrowing the mission, you can concentrate your energies, focus your embellishments, and multiply your opportunities to excel.

8 It's orderly.

The color scheme dictates a clean, uncluttered look that organizes the room around it, and organizes your head. In a fast-moving world of sensory overload—flashing electronics, fad-based advertisements, and family and work responsibilities—the simple colors and lines of the black and white room allow you to streamline your downtime surroundings.

9 It's calming.

Like sugar, too much color is exciting for a moment and then draining. Humans have been programmed for millennia to be jolted by a dash of red: Look! A sweet berry in a dark green tree! The nervous system registers excitement at first, but too much can take its toll over time. The black and white palette rests the senses.

10 It's liberating.

By maintaining a hard line palettewise from the beginning, you can move forward without paralyzing indecision. The "paradox of choice"—that too many options freeze decision-making—is the essential problem of decorating in today's world.

ageless rooms

LEFT

A fireside grouping of white upholstered chairs—set in contrast to a complex geometric rug and bold and dark canvases—gives the eye a perfect island of crisp, patternless refuge.

RIGHT

Strict adherence to black, white, and gray makes an array of patterns, from zigzag and chevrons to trellis, snakeskin, and graphic numeric plates, cohesive rather than dizzying.

ABOVE LEFT
Glossy black paint is the perfect
backdrop for a medley of artwork and
bathroom necessities.

ABOVE RIGHT
Black and white marble floors, an ebony
sideboard, and patinated dark leather
bring distinction to one of a home's
trickiest spots to decorate: the "what
goes below" a staircase's slanting wall.

RIGHT
This photo has been pinned above
my desk for years as a reminder of
the majesty that can be achieved
with a simple black and white striped
wallpaper.

ABOVE LEFT
Bunny Williams upholstered the walls
in an alternating matte and shiny
striped silk to make this dining room
formal, but still cozy.

ABOVE RIGHT
Dramatic black and gold millwork
frames a succession of classically
designed rooms by Neal Stewart,
pulling the eye deeper and deeper into
the house.

RIGHT
Jeffery Bilhuber's deft hands
harmonize tribal, Art Deco, and
modern shapes in black, white, and
various wood tones.

Black walls and white upholstery
emphasize the architecture, gilt work,
chinoiserie screens, and pastoral depth
of a large painting in this 1980s design
by Mark Hampton.

OPPOSITE

Gray weathered shingles, trellising, and patchworked wood planks offer a faded natural integrity to the sharp white of trimwork, planters, outdoor furniture, and floral blooms.

ABOVE

Black and white striped siding, curtains, and outdoor cushions set a fanciful stage for two white busts in an inviting setting by Mary McDonald.

Though this photograph was taken
sixteen years ago, gallerist Roger
Lussier's living room still feels timeless
thanks to well-chosen antiques,
different values of cream, white,
and gilt, and simple rod-and-pocket
unlined silk curtains.

nailing the palette

Here's my secret for choosing a palette and knowing pretty well what the results will be: When I'm trying out different colors, I always sample at least four shades of white or black, painting two coats of each candidate on foam core or posterboard so that I can move it around the room, seeing how the hue looks in shadowy corners and in light-saturated focal points. Take these extra steps; mistakes are costly and it would be a shame to live with something less than ideal, particularly after the years of dreaming that go into most home improvement projects. And be sure to take into account the elements of a room that are outside of your control: The extreme white of a porcelain sink can make white walls look yellow or gray, for example, so in a bathroom, start with the realities of your fixtures before hunting down the ideal paint chip.

While manipulating these colors may sound commensurate with the headache of matching a new coverlet to an existing sheet set, the results are well worth the extra homework involved. But before you head out to the paint store, keep reading: The following chapter offers a crash course on basic design principles that will inform your decision-making process and help you deploy your color scheme with the greatest of ease—and to the best effect.

OPPOSITE
Single notes of black, white, and, in this case, dog amplify Keith Brown's considered use of light in this luminous entry: The white marble floor and gloss paint finish literally glow.

My Go-to White and Black Paint Colors

I rarely use the same color twice because of the differences in natural and artificial light, but I've come to rely on a certain set of whites and blacks.

BLACKS

benjamin moore's carbon copy: Infused with a violet undertone, this is slick, glossy, and cool.

farrow & ball's off-black 57: Very dark but a little soft, which means it plays well with other colors.

farrow & ball's railings 31: This has a subtle hint of brown, so I call it "old park bench black."

benjamin moore's soot: As the name suggests, the underlying theme here is gray and blue, making for a moodier paint shade.

pratt & lambert's old mystic: It's an olive black, but I use it as though it's pitch-black.

benjamin moore's night shade: This has the subtlest tinge of aubergine.

benjamin moore's black bean soup: This is a great brown black.

fine paints of europe's #167: This is my go-to paint brand for an exquisite high-gloss finish. I've found it's the best way to achieve a lacquerlike effect.

ralph lauren's bone black th16: For those who want the "blackest black."

WHITES

benjamin moore's white dove: A hint of cream makes this my favorite white when I want some warmth.

benjamin moore's super white: My whitest white. Highly reflective, great for floors. Doesn't compete; lets other colors be "true." My go-to ceiling and molding color in modern spaces.

benjamin moore's linen white: Absolutely classic. A bit warm and not overly crisp, meaning it never looks brand-new. Fades into the background, offering support to the other colors in the room. My kitchen cabinets are linen white, since I wanted the room to look lived in instantly. It's convenient that many brands of tiles, window shades, and premade woodwork come matched to this color.

farrow & ball's pointing 2003: This is a warm and enveloping neutral that I would use on walls in the "estate emulsion" finish for a chalky look.

the rollinson collection's calm: This is an ethereal, very pale gray that is slightly warm and best in a matte finish for a soft glow. I would use it on walls or consider it for a ceiling, since it's neutral enough.

fine paints of europe's #2, #5, #17: As they did with black, they nail the high-gloss finish. It's pricey but worth it.

benjamin moore's mascarpone (from the affinity color collection): A tiny bit trendier than its other white counterparts, this shade is a touch cool.

Finding Harmony in an All-White Room

Sonu Mathew, an in-house interior designer for Benjamin Moore, is a professional ponderer of color palettes. According to Mathew, there's a current penchant for washing an entire room in a single shade. This risks depriving a room of depth and contrast, however, and the eye will have nowhere to rest. For instance, if you use the exact same paint for the molding and the walls, you may imagine they will blend beautifully. In reality, harmony comes from playing tones off each other. In an all-white room, use a palette of a light, medium, and dark shades of white, in varying doses of cool and warm. (Favorites for this task are the grayish Collingwood; White Heron, which is bright, with touches of blue; and Evening White, tinged with warm, pink undertones.) The floor takes the darker white, the medium white is designated for the walls, and the lightest white goes on the moldings and ceilings.

2 THE BASICS OF GOOD DESIGN
tools for getting black and white right

"If you want to make beautiful music, you must play the black and white notes together."
—Richard Nixon

IN 1955 THE RENOWNED industrial designer Dieter Rams joined the (then little-known) German electronics company Braun as an architect and interior designer. Though originally charged with expanding the company's campus, within a few years he was reconceiving and developing its entire product line, turning out iconic and impeccably designed stereos, coffeemakers, and alarm clocks. He also created Vitsoe, a sleek, modular shelving system that remains unchanged from its inception in 1959 and never looks jarring even in spaces that have a more traditional, warm design ethos.

Despite his remarkable success creating products and furniture, Rams's most enduring legacy is his ten principles of design, which are still taught in art schools across the world. He demanded that design be

1 honest

2 unobtrusive

3 useful

4 illuminating

5 aesthetically pleasing

6 innovative

7 thoroughly detailed

8 long-lasting

9 environmentally friendly (well ahead of his time)

10 "as little design as possible"

Whether you adopt all of Rams's rules or not, there's a lot to take away from his vision of precision and perfection, in which everything that's required is there, and nothing more. This is particularly appropriate when reimagining rooms in a pared-down, black and white palette, where the contrast in the colors has an almost architectural function, making the room's lines visible and exposing design flaws. It sounds intimidating, but this is precisely why it's such a rewarding challenge to design with this duo: The mistakes can't be fudged, and the successes stand out gloriously.

the interior speaks

These are some of my favorite examples of successful black and white design schemes—for four varied aesthetics.

ABOVE

Laura Day's use of white shaggy carpet, clear-glass accents, and graphic trellis paper make this room light, fresh, and mod.

RIGHT

The ultimate, timeless foyer: Black-and-white photography covers a white wall over a curved staircase that spills onto a checkered floor.

LEFT
Gray balloon shades languorously hang in Axel Vervoordt's dining room where modest cream-painted floors bracket a soaring white-framed mirror and vase collection.

BELOW
The nautilus-like shape of this sinuous marvel of a staircase sweeps the eye downward in this Cullman Kravis–designed town house.

THIS PAGE

White and chrome *everything* allows the scale and shape of Gary Hutton's design choices to stand in quiet, angular perfection beneath statement-making (to say the least) art.

OPPOSITE

Joel Woodard demonstrates the most "manly use" of chintz I've ever seen. A charcoal-toned Albert Hadley fabric, reintroduced by F. Schumacher, dresses a window, while charcoal walls stand above crisscross-patterned painted floors.

Creams, whites, naturals, and shots of black and charcoal highlight the sculptural forms of furniture and architectural elements. This gentle palette warms both of these modern but beautifully eclectic spaces by Gary Spain (above), and Thomas O'Brien (left).

ABOVE
Framed by black walls, dramatic art and pillows (crafted from vintage Pucci scarves) have the impact of a sonic boom in Amy Lau's mod design.

RIGHT
In Rita Konig's living room, the layered accessories, patterns, and art collections take the gray and white palette in a cozy direction, while the clean lines of the coffee table pull the room toward a more modern sensibility.

Jennifer Post underscores the
geometries of her upholstered pieces
with dark wood frames and contrasting
welting. This room achieves a balance
of sophistication and simplicity that
makes it a perfect example of the
power of a black and white pairing.

Don't Be Trite

It's essential to be thoughtful when you're planning to make over a room in a black and white palette. It's not that the colors themselves speak so loudly, but how you deploy them matters. Ambitious decorators need to keep in mind the uniquely communicative powers of black and white décor. Because it can say so much, you need to be sure your room says the *right* thing, and also take care not to put your space in the sad position of repeating easy black and white clichés. There's nothing particularly characterful about putting a black chest in a TV room with a white carpet and a twill-covered futon, but it's far worse to splash out on a Hallmark card's idea of luxe—a show-offy grand piano accessorized with a glass of champagne, a bud vase, perhaps a white Persian kitten. . . . To be sophisticated in your black and white design takes forethought and courage as well as a collection of distinctively shaped furnishings and a complexity of fabric patterns.

In Michelle Nussbaumer's balanced hands, a very controlled palette of black, white, and taupe allows myriad patterns and chinoiserie elements to soar with fantastic whimsy.

black and white gestures

For a strong overall visual statement, you can be daring, or you can make a cautious initial commitment. Black and white doesn't have to be a grand, all-encompassing concept; you will find that you can add movement and boldness to your space with small, well-chosen gestures.

THE SMALL GESTURE

- Confine your black and white stripe to a mudroom or side entrance hall.
- Hang a big white plaster-framed mirror in your entryway.
- Curate a grouping of black objects.
- Have an old ottoman or chair cushion upholstered in a graphic black and white fabric, or upholster a chair or a couch in black—with crisp white piping.
- Have your all-white towels embroidered with a black monogram.
- Switch out your tired lampshades for black string shades or your chandelier shades to black paper.
- Lacquer your front door black.

OPPOSITE

In Lela Rose's living room, the unifying element of simple black frames generates a mesmerizing crawl of black-and-white photography that leads the eye from the white epoxy floors all the way up to the ceiling.

ABOVE

There are small but decisive touches you can adopt to ease yourself into the black and white aesthetic, like the spirit-lifting, clean embrace of a wrought-iron bed in Dara Caponigro's mostly white room.

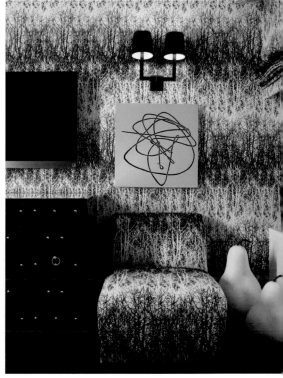

OPPOSITE
This room by Nathan Egan Interiors feels like an optical illusion as large black-and-white graphics pulse with Pop Art energy.

ABOVE
In a wallpaper by F. Schumacher, strands of birch silhouette wrap the walls. A coordinating fabric on the roman shade and upholstery envelope this media room in a branchy thicket.

THE GRAND GESTURE

- Use the same black and white fabric on your walls, curtains, and upholstery.

- Paint your window frames, moldings, and door black (balanced by a stark white wall).

- Paint wide diagonal stripes on your floor, or an oversize checkerboard print that's slightly more subversive than traditional.

- Any wall treatment in black is dramatic, but if you want the grandest of gestures, try black lacquer, upholstered silk velvet, or plaster.

ABOVE
The black end-cap on this classic banister is the perfect punctuation of a black dotted "i".

RIGHT
In a New York City powder room, a woven wall upholstery fabric in a modern damask pattern softens the austerity of otherwise black marble walls.

LEFT

A horizontal strié pattern on a black high-gloss wall is reflective enough to mirror and dramatize the Lucite and brass sculpture in the foreground—and is a nice counterpoint to the linenlike texture on the bright white loveseat.

BELOW

A long Parsons-style bench banded in black and white mimics the effect of the staircase's alternating black and white risers and treads in designer Nicole Yee's Maine summer home.

modern design: the items traditionalists can embrace

There are elements of modern design that I think work well as versatile building blocks or delightful counterpoints regardless of the prevailing design ethic. Here are some of my favorites:

1 Saarinen tables.

2 Lucite or lacquer anything, from a small keepsake box to a bedside table.

3 Leather-covered and stitched furniture (look to Jacques Adnet) or parchment-finished items.

4 Parsons or waterfall-shaped coffee or console tables.

5 Slipper chairs.

6 Modern art or modern framing on traditional art.

7 A tall clean-lined metal étagère.

8 Modern undecorated curtain hardware with self-returns (no finials).

9 Danish mid-century consoles.

10 A floating shelf (professionally installed!).

11 Twentieth-century Venetian glass (Barovier & Toso, Venini Mazzega, or Seguso).

Situated against a sueded wall, a hard, liquidlike Lucite console adds extreme textural contrast. Lucite and glass materials are a modern update on a traditional Louis XVI shape.

The minimal lines of a sleek black Parsons table allow the shape of the table lamps, box collection, and wall arrangement to define the setting.

traditional design: the items modernists can embrace

Traditional decorative elements can be used to modern ends. Here are a few that can stand in without corrupting the clarity of modern design.

1   Cast-stone tree pots.

2   Asian-style cocktail tables.

3   A carved-gilt-framed mirror.

4   Napoleon III furniture.

5   A tiny bit of trompe l'oeil trickery (at a minimum to hide vents, switch plates, and such).

6   A ceramic or stone garden stool.

7   White plaster decorative elements.

8   A folding screen to soften a corner or hide clutter.

OPPOSITE
Though this Timothy Whealon–designed bedroom has no molding and a modern fireplace, warm whites, a reflective mirror, lacquer finishes, and a screen soften the lines and make the overall effect serene.

BELOW
Nothing is more old-school traditional than a silhouette portrait. Grouped en masse, they become less sentimental and more resonant and graphic.

the perfectly imperfect floorplan

ABOVE
Tom Scheerer makes room for a pull-up chair in this sweet island bedroom. Regardless of size, I think a seating option other than the bed is a basic floor-plan necessity in every bedroom.

OPPOSITE
Although this is a large house in Litchfield County, Connecticut, Michael Leva balances larger upholstery pieces with the elegant taper of a pair of klismos chairs. A profusion of clean lines and leggy pieces put the priority on the decorative objects.

An ideal floorplan on paper might just feel far from natural in real life. When you draw up plans for a new space, try to respect the sense of proportion and the navigational patterns that are hardwired into the human psyche and the natural world. Adrian Zecha, the founder of the luxurious and lovely Aman Resorts, adjusted to this law long ago. When he chooses a location for a resort, he takes note of the paths and shortcuts that are worn into the land, and pays attention to how the locals—including the goats—access the beach and navigate the hills. Even if the routes seem counterintuitive, he incorporates them into his plan. And when the seasons change, it becomes clear that the seemingly more direct paths get washed away in floods every spring, or lie on shifting, shaky shale. There's a logic to the natural flow of traffic.

This is a good lesson to apply as we create the floorplans for our living spaces: When you arrange your furniture according to an ideal, be realistic and practical about that ideal. Just because you have a two-thousand-square-foot loft to fill doesn't mean that you should place your coffee table four feet from the sofas and chairs. It might seem more logical on an architectural plan, but it's not conducive to living, to resting your feet or your drink.

The height of a table, the depth of a seat, the distance of knee to cocktail table, the placement of an armchair in natural light have commonsense guidelines. If you disobey them in a quest for innovation, you'll probably find that your family and your guests don't *like* your new room.

If you have a house or an apartment with small rooms, don't overcrowd them, as if the walls were wider than they are. The room will feel bigger if you size its furnishings appropriately. And even if your home is large, blocking its superhighways (from the sofa to the refrigerator, for example) with misplaced furniture will make your existence uncomfortable.

creating space in your designs

Pruning your color choices will unclutter your space to some extent, but if you are someone who dislikes a minimalist aesthetic, and you prefer the humanizing "moss" of life—small tables, footstools, pillows, wall hangings, cachepots, books, small and tall lamps, sculptures, paintings, and so on—you may find you need to prune your furnishings, too. In order for light and shadow to interplay, enough free space must be available for them to work against and with one another.

In any room, however multilayered, keep at least one horizontal and one vertical surface clean and uncluttered to help maintain the right balance. Apply symmetry throughout the room, and then designate a separate table to bear the bulk of decorative objects. If that table is quickly subsumed, use your walls as a catchall, but resist the urge to blanket every surface with items.

RIGHT
In a white space, darker furniture islands ground the room. Although there are many accessories present, simple white walls and the careful placement of a few eye-catching, large-scale decorative objects make for a room that feels collector-like, but not too crowded.

OPPOSITE
Another space with many defining accessories, this living room remains orderly due to the relaxing repetition of symmetry. Only one rogue black ottoman throws the near-perfect balance a touch askew.

tricks for threading
a room together

When you're decorating in color, it's easy to disguise modest furniture or architecture with eclectic and exuberant shades and textures. But when you choose to abandon the camouflage that color offers and rely solely on black and white, you need to take special care to vary texture, shapes, styles, and periods to keep the design lively and interesting. In creating a variety of shades and ideas for the eye to ponder, you will keep your design from looking flat, like a page in a catalog.

Enlisting a variety of aesthetics doesn't mean that your space will look like an off-kilter smorgasbord. When I consider the most stylish women I

LEFT

In this family room, cheeky leopard-dot wallpaper gives spirit to a space built around the principle of "make it washable, or forget about it." Elements include kids-friendly black Flor tile carpet and the unblemishable plastic Saarinen table and chairs.

RIGHT

This beautiful white room traced in ornate molding is grand in scale but anchored by a black fireplace, a charcoal English arm sofa, a zebra rug, and the beautiful collections of owners John Dransfield and Geoffrey Ross. I especially love the big-skirted table, which softens the expanse of ebonized wood floor.

OPPOSITE

A white and mod-yellow color scheme makes for a bright and energetic bedroom.

LEFT

Antique chairs, natural sisal carpet, and a zebra rug warm this white bedroom. Swapping out the throw pillows and blanket would make this room feel entirely different when the whim strikes.

BELOW

A turquoise banquette and blue-framed mirror create the focal point in this otherwise black and white dining room.

know, I'm hard-pressed to find one who painstakingly coordinates her outfits. Back home in Palm Beach, there are plenty of ladies whose hot-pink sun hats just happen to match their nail polish and the jauntily tied sweater on their shoulders, but my friends in New York knit together chic ensembles that work in more subtle, sleight-of-hand ways. Usually there's a unifying thread that brings the look together, whether it's an underlying aesthetic or a subtly punctuating color. Maybe the red of a skirt is picked up by an earring carved to resemble a lion's head, with a ruby set in its mouth; or a cerulean blouse is mimicked by one bead on a twenty-stone necklace. Somehow, there's just enough repetition of a theme to create harmony.

Unifying factors are important in rooms, too. White—unless it's the main statement—is so predominant that it disqualifies itself as the element that imposes order. Even a few moments of black supply meaningful structure. If you have wood furniture in discordant species or finishes, think about quickly restaining all of it in the same wash. Using shots of gray—stone-hued paint, a dove-colored pillow, a collection of silver vases, a steel lamp—is a subtle but strong alternative. And finally, color is a visually muscular organizer: A few dots of red, or bright blue, or Kelly green can be all you need, assuming you're starting from a place of primarily black and white.

using black and white to assess a room's success

Every interior designer knows that there are times when a room just isn't working—something is jarring, or subtly off, and you just can't figure out exactly what's throwing the ship off balance. The best trick for this sort of impasse is to take a photo of the room and flip it upside down, at which point the flaws usually make themselves abundantly clear. Looking at the inverted photo, you realize that the curtains are too high or too low, or that the sofa is slightly off-center. Isolating the fundamentals of the design by making them unrecognizable is incredibly clarifying.

Similarly, I've taken to photographing my more colorful rooms in black-and-white, so I can get a sense of the various gradations at play. It's an excellent way to assess whether the colors are all too middle-tone, or too stark and high-contrast. Taking away the distraction of color helps the eye make a quicker judgment about other elements.

DEBUNKING BLACK AND WHITE MYTHS

Black and white are more loaded, both culturally and scientifically, than any other color pairing. Here, the two most common misconceptions:

myth Black paint will make a room feel claustrophobic.

reality Black can make a room feel larger by eliminating its edges.

how to use it to your advantage My friend Bronson Van Wyck, an in-demand event designer, often paints the ceiling black when he's designing a party space, since it creates the illusion of an infinite sky. This trick is also commonly used in theaters and in furniture and clothing showrooms, since it magnifies the perceived height of the ceiling without drawing attention away

from the action on the floor. Use high-gloss black to make a tiny room dressy or put black patent leather on the ceiling of a small entry or powder room.

———————

myth White makes a room feel large and airy.

reality An empty, white-walled apartment can feel as cramped as a dorm room, especially when the walls run into one another with no distinguishing architectural details.

how to use it to your advantage Include darker elements to anchor the space so your eye can judge the distances "to and from." Otherwise, all the white planes and materials converge, making the room feel small and shrunken.

3 DECORATING WITH EMOTION
letting your interiors speak for you

"Light is meaningful only in relation to darkness, and truth presupposes error. It is these mingled opposites which people our life, which make it pungent, intoxicating. We only exist in terms of this conflict, in the zone where black and white clash."

—Louis Aragon

The use of Rorschach inkblots as art inspires musings about the complexity of individual perception and the line between art and decorative object, and encourages a simple appreciation for their depictive beauty.

I ALWAYS THINK the strongest design schemes combine a coherent aesthetic vision with a client's genuine, individualized passions and tastes. Whether you prefer Bohemia to Park Avenue, swirling op-art murals to sharp Serra sculptures, or velvet Art Nouveau chaises to Eames chairs, the sensibility and the canvas are yours to bring together. A black and white palette can be your own design Rorschach and mean what *you* want it to mean.

Though I'm known for traditional (or neo-traditional) design schemes, I try to mix it up. Any time you adhere too intensely to an aesthetic, you run a significant risk of painting yourself into a corner. What happens when you fall in love with an intricate turn-of-the-century chair that just doesn't jibe with your ultramodern furnishings? It's much easier in the long run to build a concept that welcomes different styles, since you don't want to burn out on a pervasive design shtick, then find yourself wanting to redecorate in a handful of years.

A balanced and fulfilling room should please each of these senses:

sight An area of intense visual excitement should be tempered by a quiet and clean spot where the eye can rest.

sound The clatter of feet on a hardwood floor is part of the tempo of life, but other areas of the home, like bedrooms and dens, should be plushly carpeted or upholstery heavy, permitting silent activity.

touch Variegated textures should please this all-important sense. Think of the smooth cool of a marble countertop, offset by a wool-clad barstool.

temperature Most rooms need the option of a cozy, insulating throw. And a northern bathroom could be enhanced with towel warmers and radiant-

heated floors. Install ceiling fans where you don't need the overhead light and use your fireplaces if you have them.

smell: Stock up on scented candles and curate your cleaning supplies—my favorite "clean smell" is Mrs. Meyer's geranium scent—or let the perfume of a spent fire pervade your living room.

sentiment Surround yourself with memory-evoking items, books, art, and pictures of loved ones. These create the "story" of your house.

ABOVE LEFT
Above a bearskin rug and darkly stained wood floor in art consultant Blair Voltz Clark's apartment, black back-painted niches hold a pair of Wonjun Choi's ethereal glue–fish skeleton sculptures, which spin on monofilament line and are spotlit by halogen bulbs. Sasha Sykes's Plexiglas cube, filled with straw stems, acts as side table next to a chalk-white settee, under a Richard Serra.

ABOVE RIGHT
This is no wallflower of a side chair thanks to a Mongolian sheep fur seat that's so absurdly fluffy it practically begs to have its ears scratched.

go bold, not boring

If you've ever taken a painting class (or become mesmerized by Bob Ross's PBS show, *The Joy of Painting*), you know how unpretty a canvas in progress can be. Usually it looks like a series of disastrous flaws or bland color blocks until you near the end, when it miraculously comes together with defining highlights and lowlights. Decorating is a similar act of faith. If you only choose the easy answers and the middle ground, your design will get boring, fast.

Assembling and designing a great house consumes so much time and energy that there can be a tendency to get a little precious about your space. It's like when you spend hours cleaning your house, and wince when someone walks across the carpet, marring the perfect stripes left behind by the vacuum. Remind yourself that rooms are for living.

Sometimes furniture doesn't fit perfectly, or materials don't match—if that happens, embrace that hiccup and force yourself to move forward to find the solution. If you're feeling timid and on the fence, keep in mind that most stores and galleries will let you take pieces on approval, so try that bold art piece or rug before you buy it: It may look awful or it might be absolutely perfect.

The approach of adapting, rather than starting afresh each time, is not only more productive, it also generates more fertile and successful designs. I find that the most interesting houses are the ones in which you can detect the journey of the design in the outcome.

In Jackson, Mississippi, Richard Keith Langham incorporated collected objects from his client's African travels in a playful, neo-Edwardian garden room.

my list: a few essentials for every home

It's different for every decorator, but these are the items I firmly believe are worth getting right for the long term. Consider them the bones that will grow old with you.

1. WELL-CONSIDERED OPEN AND CONCEALED SHELVING

Shelving is interior architecture: Whether you choose custom, built-in, mill-work cabinets, or a more modular approach, it's key to provide enough space to accommodate your life. Even if you're not an avid reader, you will most definitely find things to fill the space over the years. Consider whether you want shelves for display, or if it's a more pressing priority for you to create concealed storage to hide your belongings. Are you an antiquist (or junkist) who celebrates the object, or a minimalist who celebrates clean space? When left to my own devices, I prefer a bit of both: Art books are meant to be admired, but I keep my paperbacks, cookbooks, and *Breastfeeding for Dummies* in cabinets.

ABOVE LEFT
The table draws you into the beautiful chaos of paper, color, and book matter. Open shelving creates library-like exposure and honors a collection of favorite classics.

LEFT
Concealed shelving in a guest room by Burnham Designs hides essentials, while a small area of open shelving allows for the display of more curated objects.

The étagère-style bookshelf showcases the texture of a Madagascar grasscloth wallpaper and lends a more open feeling to this loft, where study and living room merge. Vintage brass bookends by Ben Seibel are practical and sculptural.

Diamond-paned leaded windows let in a flood of light across neatly stacked art books.

2. SOMETHING SALVAGED

I love to search through architectural salvage shops for old doors, shutters, flooring, and double-paned windows (make sure you add a UV film to protect your furnishings from the sun). Salvaged goods can add great patina, and are often much more interesting—and sometimes even lower priced—than new items on the market. If your doors and moldings are standard-issue, try painting them a glossy black to add gravitas, or hunt for a magnificent old door-knocker and an oversize knob. Reclaimed wood flooring is a great option in new spaces; not only are you recycling, but you're getting something perfectly worn in, which will make the house feel unique.

LEFT
In this butler's pantry, Gail Plechaty installed a functional antique cabinet that has far more character than a new built-in one would have.

ABOVE
A salvaged wood floor in a chevron pattern adds so much soul that this bedroom feels beautifully composed, even with bare white walls and a simple sheeted bed.

3. DISTINCTIVE MOLDING

Often thought of as an ornate element, molding actually serves a utilitarian
purpose—it's traditionally used as a Band-Aid to cover the inevitable shifting
between floors and walls, or poor workmanship. Wood flooring naturally
expands and contracts seasonally, so it usually needs about half an inch vari-
ance from where it hits the walls, which molding covers. Ceilings are rarely
level, so both houses and apartment buildings shift constantly. Applying horizontal molding can disguise this. Molding is worth the splurge. It's an almost
essential fixture if you want to use wallpaper, and it makes a house look infi-
nitely more "finished." And from a style point of view, unless your home is
deliberately ultramodern, the absence of moldings produces the sad effect of a
suit without a belt.

4. LAYERS OF LIGHTING

During renovations or new construction, carefully think through all components of lighting and outlet placement at the outset. Consider where you want overhead lighting or chandeliers, sconces, and lamps. Light should come from more than two heights in any room. Though you can run a cord from anywhere and conceal it with a rug, placing outlets in the floor is a lot more elegant and less intrusive. And remember to tape the cords to the back legs of your table or under a nearby sofa skirt if the base of the table is exposed.

5. PERSONAL ART

Art collecting is a very personal process, but you can start at any time, regardless of budget. I picked up some of my favorite works at flea markets for less than what I spent on snacks. If you're at the higher end of the spectrum, talk with art consultants about your desires—they often have access to pieces, galleries, and ideas that will help you make the most informed decision possible. And when you fall in love with a piece, their expertise can enhance your confidence and commitment.

6. STRIKING MARBLE

Either as a tabletop, coffee table, mantel, or windowsill, a single great slab of rock will last forever and lend a room material variety, subtle pattern, and a bit of grandeur. While shopping for coffee tables and side tables, I often focus on the bases more than the tops, knowing I can cover them with marble or mirror.

OPPOSITE
Black high-gloss walls look lacquerlike behind Carson Fox's fantastical resin-cast flower work, *Scope Blue,* and reference the Nero marble cabochons in a diamond-pattern pillowed Carrera floor.

ABOVE
Striking inky veining dashes across a marble bartop–breakfast nook overlooking the Hudson River. Harlem toile wallpaper by Sheila Bridges takes a celebratory tone behind framed Emancipation Era black-and-white etchings.

7. DISTINCTIVE KNOBS AND HARDWARE

These are an instant upgrade on furniture pieces, cabinetry, or doors that would otherwise scream standard-issue. You can easily take them with you if you move.

8. AN ANTIQUE MIRROR

Both soulful and poetic, an antique mirror is a must for every home. You can never have enough items that are already aged: They don't wear or decay the way something new would. Your local glass shop can also produce a very good faux-antiqued mirror and add it to glass-fronted cabinets or install it in an antique frame.

9. SOMETHING ALIVE

Greenery may eventually die, but it never goes out of style. If you can't keep your trees alive, invest in a planter you love, and just live with the expectation of filling it a few times a year with a new victim until you learn better habits or meet something you can't kill. Good fake trees and the odd fake plant are not unforgivable design faux pas, but really good ones are harder to find than cheap white truffles out of season. Choose plants that naturally look a bit waxy, such as succulents, orchids, olive trees, and fiddle fig trees to pull off the illusion most successfully. Avoid anything that might appear in your doctor's office or nail salon.

10. A SILVER FRAME COLLECTION

I use these to hold black-and-white photos, for an easy, graceful, and timeless statement. They blend well together as you slowly collect them over time (search flea markets, eBay, etc.).

11. DISTINCTIVE DETAILS

Don't underestimate the effect of decorative trim. It can anchor a skirt or highlight the unexpected lines of a valance.

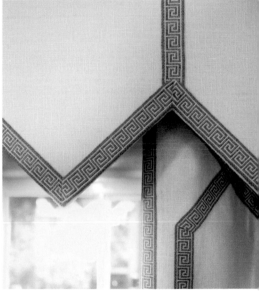

ABOVE
Tiny Greek-key tape trim highlights the valance shape on a cream-colored linen; black-and-white tape trim adds grounding to the base of a skirted sofa.

4 LOOKING FOR INSPIRATION black and white in nature, hollywood, and beyond

"I often think that the night is more alive and more richly colored than the day."

—Vincent Van Gogh

A Holstein cow, a guinea feather, the night sky, driftwood, quail eggs, birch trees, obsidian, glistening dewdrops on a spider's web: They all bring to mind a favorite poem, "Pied Beauty," by Gerard Manly Hopkins.

Glory be to God for dappled
   things—
For skies of couple-color as a
   brindled cow;
For rose-moles all in stipple upon
   trout that swim;
Fresh-firecoal chestnut-falls; finches'
   wings;
Landscape plotted and pieced—fold,
   fallow, and plough;
And all trades, their gear and tackle
   trim.

All things counter, original, spare,
   strange;
Whatever is fickle, freckled (who
   knows how?)
With swift, slow; sweet, sour;
   adazzle, dim;
He fathers-forth whose beauty is
   past change:
Praise him.

ONE OF THE THINGS I dislike about life in New York City is that thanks to the overwhelming amount of light pollution, you never really get to see the night sky, to feel its infinite depth. But, as a consolation, I get to take in a different set of stars, for every evening, a million office and apartment lights twinkle against a deep black horizon. Anybody who has flown over Manhattan under the dark embrace of a velvety night understands how stunning—and glamorous—that cityscape can be.

This is a lesson worth bringing indoors: Just as darkness sets off the stars and the moon, a room needs punctuation, highlights, and contrasting borders to evoke the natural counterpoint that all of us respond to. Nature provides a rich concert of harmonious oppositions. Have you ever looked at a broad snow-covered slope—dotted with dark boulders, a falling-down fence, or a lone pine tree—and noticed the striking gradations of tone that give the view resonance and depth? Or have you walked alongside a broad Hawaiian lava field, undulant with basalt waves that glint in the sunlight?

Think about how this clarity of contrast is so revealing in black-and-white photos, as well as in old Hollywood film sets. At a wedding, the bride's white gown and the groom's black tuxedo set them apart from the guests who surround them in rowdier colors. Afterward, in photographs, the man in black and the woman in white emerge as the cornerstone of the vivid assemblage—the obvious subject. Black and white *is* memory. Anyone who's ever watched a colorized version of *Casablanca* knows how disappointing it is to see your nostalgic recollections of the film diluted and blurred in a wash of unmemorable color. Time goes by in color; we remember it in black and white.

Even if you're dedicated to enforcing a strict all-white design, you must create moments of punctuating shadow and relief—your whites are only

Soot marks the escape of smoke from
the fireplace while a low-slung bed
faces off against a high ceiling.

white in comparison to the darkest objects in the room. These small moments of drama, which will make the architecture and nuances of your space sing, hinge on gradation, however subtle. Resist the temptation to wash the walls, ceiling, and trim of your room in the same shade of paint, for example; it will look flat and dull, rather than quietly vibrant. You can create harmony without relying on homogeny. After all, homogeny doesn't exist in nature—and what feels and looks natural generally looks right.

ABOVE

In this Libby Cameron–designed room, the twinkling of the city skyline steps in as the understudy for stars that are lost in light pollution.

RIGHT

Dappled with sun, Dara Caponigro's attic room is cloudlike, complete with the gauziest of sheets and softest punctuations of shadow.

bringing nature home

Many people these days are rejecting the sterility of excessively modern décors and actively inviting nature into their homes, or building their homes around nature. In our kitchens, by our hearths, in our bedrooms and dens, we can display boulders, marble tabletops, plank floors, shells, feathers, fur, animal portraits, wall paintings of the cosmos, and even living trees.

At one extreme of the nature-meets-design spectrum there's Frank Lloyd Wright's famous house Fallingwater, in western Pennsylvania. The low-ceilinged and plentifully windowed house straddles a stream and a waterfall, and appears to grow organically out of its woodsy surroundings. But you don't have to buy a hillside and hire a paradigm-shifting architect to make a powerful statement about your reverence for the natural world. Nature offers many forms of black-and-white inspiration, from cumulus clouds to herds of grazing Angus cows. Bringing the outside world indoors can be accomplished through subtle touches, or in more dramatic ways.

LEFT

A black and white document print with a toile-style effect is overpinned with actual insects, creating an entomologist's kaleidoscope-like fantasy in Brad Ford's stunning hallway design.

OPPOSITE

Urban views interact with decorative elements that reference a different kind of jungle. The shape of the chair reminiscent of an antelope, a leather-bound sisal rug, Ultrasuede walls, a raw-wood drum table, a shaggy fur pillow, and a meandering framed river map create a calming, sun-drenched nook.

QUICK-AND-EASY WAYS TO CAPTURE THE ELEMENTS

1 Layer a trellis against a mirrored ceiling and conjure the sunlit, breezy feeling of a gazebo.

2 Paint a living room wall slate or indigo to evoke the serenity and power of a nighttime ocean. Meanwhile, cream-colored, textured flooring in a breezeway or a corridor can summon the sensation of a sandy beach.

3 With a projection lamp, or with stencils (and a ladder), throw stars on the ceiling and walls of a child's bedroom, surrounding him in the glowing mystery of the Milky Way.

4 Channel the effect of a cloudy sky by hanging a cumulus-like lighting fixture, or use a pierced paper lampshade. The perforations cast shards of light and shadow on the walls. Make sure you use a clear-glass bulb so that the effect of light through the punctures is as dramatic as possible.

5 Bring the forest inside by using slender saplings for your four-poster bed, rough-cast cedar as a hallway bench, or river stones for a breeze-way floor.

6 Imitate the luster of moonlight with an opalescent lamp, or glaze your windows with hand-blown glass to recall the dappled light that the sun casts as it shines through a forest canopy or glances off a moving stream.

7 Don't disguise the tree: Choose a table that looks like a slice of a trunk—its ragged, cracked top held together with iron rivets; or rough-hewn ceiling beams that expose the tree's grained core; or a table lamp hewn from a chunk of petrified wood.

8 Introduce tiger velvet pillows, zebra rugs, tortoiseshell finishes, and faux-coral objects.

9 If you have a picturesque view, put a big mirror opposite your window and you'll get it twice.

10 Consider a pickled wood wall finish, which feels natural and soft.

11 Don't discount vintage taxidermy. There's something redemptive about finding a poor deer head in a dusty antique shop and giving it proper respect and reverence in a clean and quiet home.

ABOVE
Philip Cooper and Sally Metcalf quote
nature directly using a birch-tree bed
frame, antler lamp, fur throw, and
horn stool in a cream-toned Montana
bedroom.

LEFT
A handmade, triangular ladder works
as an unexpected and organic sky-high
headboard.

LOOKING FOR INSPIRATION   93

ABOVE LEFT
The sweet forms of a handmade basket
and bucket add a rough-hewn but
graceful counterpoint to an unadorned
and angular fireplace.

ABOVE RIGHT
Lisa Jackson uses a cylindrical metal
grate chandelier to throw dappled light
across this rustic and romantic dining
room. This effect does not work with
frosted lightbulbs; make sure to use
clear glass for spectacular shadow and
light effects.

OPPOSITE
White stoneware and a vintage enamel
factory-style pendant light break
up the otherwise woodsy feel of a
charming country kitchen.

THE HEARTH OF THE HOME

The most traditional way to imbue a room with the evocative power of the elements is to build it around a fireplace. Nothing short of the ocean or flowing water is as mesmerizing. In certain parts of the world—places with arid, desert climates or gentle winters—grand homes traditionally contain a marble courtyard with a burbling fountain at the center and tall fruit trees climbing into the open sky. In colder climates, this feature is impractical, so it's the hearth where we give nature fullest rein. The crackle and scent of burning logs—in whatever season—transports everyone outside of themselves, to the realm of the wild. If a wood-burning fireplace isn't an option in your building, new fireplace technology can bring the element into your walls without violating code. The moody effects of a flame are the same whether they come from a stack of cedar logs, denatured alcohol, or a gas-fed bar.

BRINGING IN A TOUCH OF WHIMSY

In Renaissance Europe, as botanists, zoologists, biologists, and explorers traveled the globe to expand their knowledge of the natural world, a vogue arose for "cabinets of curiosities." Homeowners used them to collect and display as many unusual, exotic, and beautiful organic artifacts as possible, so that they and their friends could marvel at the profusion of nature's bounty. If you have a taste for caprice, and a little imagination, you can quote literally from nature by integrating animal, vegetable, and mineral accessories into your home. Against an uncluttered, clean-lined backdrop, talismans like driftwood benches, antler chandeliers, sheepskin poufs, and zebra rugs stand out, rich in association with the world outside.

One potential pitfall of modern and even traditional black and white design is that if it's implemented too strictly, you can end up with an arid, stiff effect. The introduction of necessarily imperfect, organic elements adds a touch of coziness, interest, and texture. Don't be afraid to add flourishes of fancy and personal taste. Like the "creative black tie" instruction that accompanies some of the liveliest party invitations, use "creative black and white" as your design mantra; it will unleash unpredictable, and rich combinations.

OPPOSITE
Zebra upholstery adds a whimsical flourish to an otherwise soft-spoken but still modern gray-scale room by Jesse Carrier.

ABOVE LEFT
The collector and the naturalist cozy up in Eddie Ross and Jaithan Kochar's cottage bathroom.

ABOVE RIGHT
A leaping horse, antler stool, and zebra-print rug feel urbane in a safari-like Laura Day entryway.

LEFT
A shell-encrusted classical bust catches the moment when dignified formality cracks itself up.

ABOVE
Felted-wool "rocks" and the sloping lines of a bonsai tree offset the architecture of a fireplace.

RIGHT
Raw wood and natural fibers like seagrass and jute join an ashy aged ceramic lamp to allay an almost ascetically minimal desk setting.

OPPOSITE
Alex Shaw punctuates white walls and unfinished, straight-laid plank floors with black doors, a Wassily chair, and exotic European mounted horns.

Photography leans casually against the wall beneath a recessed flat-screen television, which looks almost like a piece of dark artwork hung deliberately above the wooden ledge. Organic modern shapes throughout the room add sculptural interest.

NATURAL COMPLEMENTS TO BLACK AND WHITE

In designing in a two-tone scheme, don't be too literal: A black and white palette won't lose thematic relevance if you incorporate natural woods, plants, sisal, sea grass, hemp, cane, rattan, grass cloth, jute, and raw linens.

ABOVE LEFT
The unfinished planks on the wall are earthy modern, not rustic. The bottom third of the chair legs call attention to themselves with raw-wood impudence.

ABOVE RIGHT
Surrounded by painted black walls, this office mixes a desk of waxed antique fruitwood, timber floors, reeded matchstick shades, and a chair of ebonized wood.

Soft-white wood paneling, naturally
occurring shapes, and organic colors
prevail in this sunroom by Brad Ford.

This black-painted room is replete with natural materials, from the textured walls and woven shades to the wooden tones throughout.

A rusted gray-painted iron bench and concrete faux-bois stool perch high above Central Park.

BELOW LEFT

Organic materials in modern but elemental shapes add sculptural and material interest to this sanctuary of a dining room.

BELOW RIGHT

A fake-fur throw warms up the foot of a bed in an all-white room.

OPPOSITE, LEFT

Organic textiles and a woven kilim rug add texture and pattern in Pam Voth's unusual dark-painted sunroom.

OPPOSITE, TOP RIGHT

A gilt mirror repeats the view of a cut-glass crystal chandelier.

OPPOSITE, CENTER RIGHT

A cluster of glass objects are airy on this countertop and offer a laboratory-like cluster that does not block the framed insects behind.

OPPOSITE, BOTTOM RIGHT

Matte-black andirons hold birch logs, the perfect wood specimen to fill a fireplace in any black and white setting.

YOUR NATURAL SHOPPING LIST

In order to reflect the manifold variety in nature, try to create a space that represents at least half of these tactile qualities.

1 **Something leather (faux or real):** an ottoman, chair, leather-wrapped furniture, bookcase interior, woven leather rug

2 **Something glimmery:** mirror or mercury glass

3 **Something crystalline:** rock crystal, Lucite, glass

4 **Something metallic:** bronze, silver, gold, nickel, copper

5 **Something woven:** straw, grass cloth, wicker, rattan, jute, sisal, Kuba cloth, seagrass

6 **Something slick:** ceramic, marble, lavastone, lacquer

7 **Something matte:** stone, wood, paint, felt

8 **Something furry:** sheepskin, Zebra or cowhide rug, fur throw or pillow. Faux can be just as nice.

drawing inspiration from black-and-white films and photographs

There's a wealth of black and white associations—some clichéd, some a bit more obscure, from the grandeur of the Kaaba or the White House to the keys of a piano or the text of a newspaper.

But most of all, the words *black and white* evoke nostalgia for cinematic romance and style, whether from classic black-and-white films like *Notorious, Some Like It Hot, My Man Godfrey,* and *The Lady Eve* or from memorable black-and-white photographs—images by Cartier-Bresson, Doisneau, and Kertész; by Capa, Avedon, and Beaton. The men and women recorded in that iconic age seem more indelible than all the faces captured on our digital cameras.

WHY BLACK AND WHITE LEAVES AN INDELIBLE MARK

The black and white home décor trend first emerged in the 1920s, thanks to Hollywood's grand arrival. If these historic glimpses speak to you in the same way, consider how you might channel the aura of those times into your own rooms.

- Try an old-fashioned pattern, such as a toile wallpaper, a chintz upholstery fabric, a houndstooth check pillow, or a herringbone floor pattern.

- Use old-fashioned shapes cast from more modern materials, such as a curving vanity mirror framed in Lucite.

- Employ something classic and loaded with connotation, like a checkerboard floor in a kitchen or an entryway.

MINING MOVIES FOR DETAILS

Without the distraction of color, the geometric forms of these cinematic designs for living are immediately apparent.

Do you want to . . . project the Art Deco sophistication of Barbara Stanwyck's cruise-ship stateroom in *The Lady Eve*?

Mimic the . . . satin comforters, antique fold-up traveling shoe case, and smooth louvered windows.

Do you want to . . . craft a space in which to entertain high-living friends in style, like the Bullocks' parlor in *My Man Godfrey*?

Mimic the . . . occasional tables and sofa disposition.

Do you want to . . . sprinkle some retro stardust into your terrace, as at The Blue Parrot and Rick's Café Américain in *Casablanca*?

Mimic the . . . potted palm, torch, and latticed screens, and you're well on your way to bringing the nostalgia back home.

5 MODERN AND GRAPHIC INTERPLAY

bordering, wall treatments, and floors

"Our lives at times seem a study in contrast . . . love and hate, birth and death, right and wrong . . . everything seen in absolutes of black and white. Too often we are not aware that it is the shades of gray that add depth and meaning to the starknss of those extremes."
—Ansel Adams

THE MOST POWERFUL FUNCTION of black and white in a design setting is their ability to create the illusion of space, to demarcate separate areas. Think of an M. C. Escher trompe l'oeil drawing: Black ink on white paper creates a labyrinth of twisting, seemingly 3-D passageways. And anybody who lovingly tangles with the daily crossword puzzle in the newspaper appreciates the contrast—the black indicating where you cannot go, and the white pointing the way ahead. The two don't exist without each other, and their relationship becomes a powerful tool when you're assembling a room. Manipulating this optical illusion in three dimensions lets you create spaces that pulsate with energy and possibilities. It's particularly pertinent when you're evaluating the framework that contains the design, that is, the walls and the floors.

RIGHT
The black stripe draws your eye upstairs in this all-white stuccoed foyer in Morocco by Popham Design.

OPPOSITE
Boldly painted molding arcs over a window to anchor the living room beneath the soaring heights of a barrel-vaulted ceiling.

the power of the silhouette

Rembrandt made his painting dramatic, chiefly through an emphatic contrast of extreme shadow with pale, luminous skin. Think of this polarity as you design a room: A dark backdrop, like a charcoal-tinted wall, accents the beautifully worked edge of an antique molding or the craftsmanship behind an intricate headboard.

Consider silhouetting by using a darker shade of the same hue, such as a blueish white behind a brighter white. Carl Minchew, a scientist who specializes in color and light at Benjamin Moore, explains that the human eye perceives a hierarchy in color tones, and will automatically single out the whitest white and the darkest dark from whatever colors fall into its field of vision. What this means is that you don't have to work quite as hard as you might imagine to create moments in your interiors, since our minds are eager to do it for us. When you're out shopping, ferret out unusual shapes, whether a pillow trimmed with tassels or an oval-shaped picture frame—breaking up the grid throws other elements into contrast.

ABOVE

The high arched sweep of a black and white–bordered headboard peaks between two heart-shaped grape-leaf fronds.

RIGHT

In this Caitlin Wilson–designed bedroom, a white headboard's black welting creates negative space against a floral Farrow & Ball wallpaper.

LEFT

Jennifer Coleman uses a graphic striped ceiling and black-on-black striped walls to create dramatic depths behind the drop of an oversize light fixture.

ABOVE RIGHT

The teapot forms of black basalt-ware stand out against cream kitchen shelves. The oval mirror behind the sink is a sweet touch.

BELOW RIGHT

A white tub stands proud in front of black wall.

trompe l'oeil:
fake it until you make it

As the Internet makes it easier and more affordable for smaller designers to enter the home design marketplace, the amount of inspired and unusual textiles and wall treatments has increased. One of my favorites of late is trompe l'oeil wallpaper, which presents the illusion of a well-stocked library of classics, or a precariously teetering stack of plates. You can also stencil your collection-to-be directly onto the wall. It's a clever solution if you lack twenty feet of books!

RIGHT

A tapering collection of travel trunk stickers dresses a white wall.

OPPOSITE

Black-and-white photographed bookshelves fill a two-dimensional wall and meet a real, three-dimensional bookcase at the corner.

A dark gray painted trellis works as applied architecture and adds an element of dynamic and unconventional door and window framing.

the room speaks: black and white wall treatments

The most expedient way to build up contrast in your home is to zero in on your walls. This is the best place to create a backdrop for the room's various silhouettes.

WHEN TO LEAVE WHITE WALLS ALONE

If the decision to leave white walls white isn't based on timidity and fear but to emphasize other elements in the room, I'm all for it. This is especially true if the rooms have distinctive architectural components that help pull it off, whether it's turn-of-the-century moldings, a tin-tile ceiling, or the seamless-ness of sleekly modern, hingeless doors.

WHEN NOT TO

If the room is a standard, unadorned box, without distinctive features, a lack of any ornament can make it feel cube-like at best; and at worst, can highlight construction flaws.

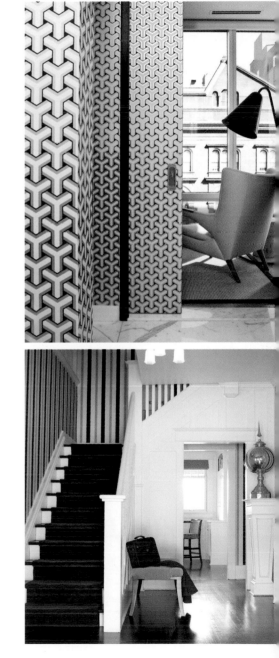

ABOVE RIGHT
Pocket doors are a great space-saving tool, but don't leave them unadorned. We opted to wallpaper these with the same design as the interior bathroom.

BELOW RIGHT
Striped wallpaper leads elegantly up a stairwell.

HOW TO OVERCOME AN OBSESSION WITH PLAIN WHITE WALLS

If you have decorated in a minimalist way in the past and find yourself squeamish about branching out into more declarative statements and design strategies, take a lesson from aversion therapy:

- Persuade yourself to paint or wallpaper one room (at the very least), and see if you find (to your surprise) that it adds satisfying depth, weight, and variation to your visual experience.

- Stick with your white but use a distinct texture, like a lacquer, pale strié, white grass cloth, a plaster treatment, or a worsted wool upholstery fabric.

HOW TO OVERCOME AN AVERSION TO WHITE WALLS

If you're a die-hard maximalist and can't imagine life outside of your tomato-red interiors, take a lesson from color therapy:

- Collect shelter magazines for a few months and rip out only photographs of rooms that you deem calming. I can almost guarantee you that the majority will be predominantly white.

- Keeping that lesson in mind, start with an all-white bedroom, where you most need visual rest, and unleash your appetite for saturated hues in the rooms with the TVs.

OPPOSITE
Black grass cloth adds warmth and texture, while tall mirrors flank an unusually high and broad window that brings light and symmetry to the room.

ABOVE
Wall decals are a fun and easily changeable option for commitment-phobes or renters.

dressing your walls

Furniture and artwork will break up the expanse of colored or textured wall that you're actually going to see. Is it stark white shelving, a long sofa, or a collection of paintings? Keep these in mind when you evaluate your treatment options.

1   Try the black wall. Painting one is a very simple, affordable way to put your toe in the water because you can always paint right over it.

2   The uptick in decal popularity is a boon for DIY-ers. Every conceivable iteration, from giant, exotic-looking trees hand-cut from wallpaper (such as Inke Heiland's) to more graphically oriented images and patterns (like those from Blik), is available.

3   You can have a custom mural printed from an extensive library of black-and-white photographs (surfaceview.co.uk).

4   Layer your walls with a textural treatment like waxed plaster, felt, burlap, or even velvet.

5   Appropriate something from the outdoors like wood planks, brick, or stone.

6   Install a giant framed tapestry, stretched like a canvas.

7   And of course, my hands-down favorite is wallpaper, though you don't have to paper an entire room—some designs are cut as a single stripe (check out the ones at thecollection.fr), or you can tackle only one wall.

ABOVE AND OPPOSITE
Cashmere blankets, swinging couches (laden with linen and velvet pillows), and ceramic-bell-hung walls create shadow, movement, and texture in this sun porch by Brad Ford.

FLAT

pros Because it reflects little light, a flat finish is good for concealing imperfections and has a classic old-world feel.

cons Arguably the most delicate of the bunch, flat-finish paint is difficult to clean and will show every scuff and fingerprint.

where to use it A low-traffic area, or on the ceiling.

WHAT'S IN A PAINT FINISH

Besides having clearly different visual qualities, finishes exist for different purposes. Here's a foolproof cheat sheet to take with you when you go to the paint store.

EGGSHELL

pros This has some of the low-sheen qualities of a flat finish, but is a bit easier to care for.

cons It's still difficult to clean and marks easily.

where to use it Almost any room, barring kid-heavy zones.

SEMIGLOSS

pros Reflects a significant amount of light and is easy to clean.

cons Reveals every imperfection in your walls, every brushstroke, and the frequent "orange-peel finish" of a roller brush.

where to use it It's ideal for doors, trim, casework, bathrooms, and kitchens. Make sure walls get a good skim coat first.

VENETIAN PLASTER

pros Often thought of as an old-school finish, if done in the right pigments and gloss, it can look modern and sleek. Wears well because the tinting runs through, so scratches and dings don't show. Higher gloss finishes wipe clean.

cons Labor intensive; best left to a professional. More difficult to paint over.

where to use it Anywhere you want a finish so special and deep, it elevates the very integrity of your wall.

HIGH GLOSS

pros A spectacular finish in rooms that are *flawlessly* skim coated. Less expensive than real lacquer (sometimes I can't tell the difference).

cons Expensive to execute well. This looks best lightly sanded between coats, and often requires six or seven turns with the brush to achieve an ideal, lacquer-like finish. The prices of the darker colors can be shocking.

where to use it Rooms that beg for drama and need to be set apart with almost special-occasion distinction, such as dining rooms, entry halls, powder rooms, and libraries.

SPECIAL FINISHES

I believe there's always room for a little extra artistry: lacquer, strié, sponge, stencil.

An interesting assemblage of objects, graphic art, and black-painted high-gloss doors makes for instant drama in Michael Bargo's apartment.

great black and white floors

When it comes to the spaces where you do most of your living—bedrooms, family rooms, dens, offices—I encourage comfort-oriented floors and putting extra priority on the tactile. No one wants to put sleepy warm feet on frigid flooring. A gorgeous industrial cement floor, stained and glossily waxed, feels cool and velvety in a hot climate but punishing in a cold one. And in rooms for children and infants, I swear by wall-to-wall carpeting: It's the greatest insurance against head bumps and the happiest surface for hours of floor play. Even if children aren't a consideration, a large area rug is a must in most bedrooms and living rooms in order to create a space that feels cozy. Feel free to layer smaller, graphic rugs on top of your larger, almost room filling, rug if it is a neutral or natural-weave rug like a sisal, sea grass, or jute.

In high-traffic areas—kitchens, bathrooms, entryways—an easy-to-clean solution is always best. Consider a patterned floor as a way to add something visually interesting, since rugs and carpets will quickly fall victim to the foot traffic in these areas. Whether you choose a classic checkerboard for the kitchen, a crisp white tile in the bathroom, or an epoxy for the entryway, floors become a significant decorative surface due to their sheer size. If I'm tiling or using a field marble, I prefer a pattern that runs on the diagonal; it's more visually arresting than a straight-line grid. I'm also a fan of wooden floors in a kitchen (they are more forgiving on legs than tile). If you have one, consider painting it; it's an easy way to get a pattern on the floor and to keep the room light and warm.

ABOVE LEFT
To create a focal point in this antechamber, Joel Woodard inlayed wood in a concentric square pattern, achieving an almost Escher-like effect.

ABOVE RIGHT
Henry Norton laid a trellis pattern with a quatrefoil center design in grays, creams, and whites in this dining room.

OPPOSITE
There are some rooms that just have charisma, and this is one of them! Philip Gorrivan's dark-painted paneling and perfectly scaled octagonal inlaid marble floor makes a small entry burst with all the energy contrast and pattern can engender.

TOP LEFT
This Lonseal vinyl floor ups the wattage of a punky, almost stylized corroded chinoiserie Mylar wallpaper.

BOTTOM LEFT
This is an unexpected spin on a traditional checkerboard floor by Cullman & Kravis and Allan Greenberg Architects.

ABOVE
Black poured-concrete tiles by Popham Design draw attention in their Marrakech courtyard.

OPPOSITE
Gary Hutton uses a dramatic variegated gray and white marble in an interlocking plank pattern in an art-filled entry.

using black and white for effective space planning

Use zones of color to block out specific task areas in a giant living space. You can create the feeling of rooms that begin and end this way—even if there are no walls at all.

Large area rugs (or pieces of bound carpet) can create pathways. Employ bookshelves and other high-backed elements as spatial dividers as well.

Use black or high-contrast items in an otherwise white or light space to create divisions in the room. Whether it's a slick low-slung credenza that separates a seating area from a dining room, or a compression shelving system that makes a transparent wall, think of these items as 2-D lines on a floorplan.

RIGHT

A swooping high-backed settee separates an intimate fireside seating area from the more well-traveled passage into the room.

FAR RIGHT

Two colors of felt wrap from floor to ceiling in Lela Rose's ovoid-shaped, New York City family room. The wall flaps ingeniously hide kids' toys and games.

A carved wooden table is an elegant addition to a large foyer; not only is it a place for display, but as an island, it creates pathway flow.

6 SHOTS OF COLOR and shades of gray

Black and white is how it should be

But shades of gray are the colors I see.

—Billy Joel

OPPOSITE

Jesse Carrier created a living room in complete gray scale: woven carpet, gray-washed coffee table, charcoal and stone wool sectional with white threaded French mattress boxing, and a black iron chandelier add an interesting range of textures and materials.

I'VE ALWAYS THOUGHT THAT the ghostlike snapshot of an X-ray is beautiful. The ash of milky gray bone—set against a darker, more impenetrable space—provides a look at our inner framework, but it also implies what is eternal, essential, and complex.

The process is similar to how a room comes together. At first it's scientifically abstract, defined by the hard frame of architecture and supporting structures, until the human elements enter in: the feeling, light, and emotion of a space.

This book has discussed—at length—how the restricted parameters of black and white can bestow the gift of clarity, but we haven't explored the limitless gradations in hue that separate the two color poles; the range of shades that bridges them is as rich and varied as the rainbow.

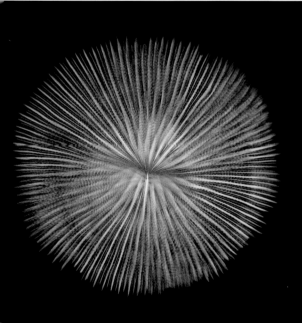
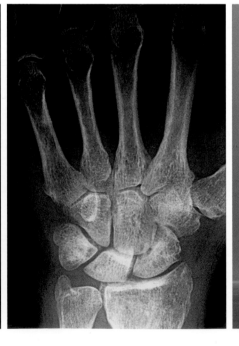

THE WAY WE LIVE
VOGUE LIVING HOUSES.GARDENS.PEOPLE

BY THE LIGHT OF THE SEA
COUNTRY LIVING
CLASSIC KITCHENS
COULEUR & HABITAT
CONTEMPORARY LIVING

decorating in gray scale

Think of a room in gray scale (meaning black, white, and everything in between) as you would think of a monochromatic outfit—say, a gray dress. With no further information, you might picture a corporate uniform: dull, austere, and gloomy. But pair that dress with a shimmery, sequined charcoal cardigan, a faded black leather jacket, and a handful of thick silver chains and you have something else entirely, something that takes minutes to decode, rather than seconds. The results can also be more tasteful and sophisticated than a similar outfit in louder colors. If you draw from too many hues in your wardrobe, you may attain Boho fabulousness—or you may find yourself costumed for the circus. The same truth applies to a room. Gray scale is markedly more flexible than colors: You can pile gray on or pare it back, and it will continue to meet the mood. The boundaries of black and white allow you to play with variety in a room, with less risk of making it look like a set from *Willie Wonka & the Chocolate Factory.*

OPPOSITE, TOP LEFT

A close-up of the many textures in the Jesse Carrier living room on page 141.

OPPOSITE, TOP RIGHT

Layered art: A bronze bust stands in the foreground while a figurative charcoal drawing cuts into the frame of a moody canvas of grays and blacks.

OPPOSITE, BOTTOM LEFT

A slightly darker wall color grounds the luminous silk of an adjacent bergere chair.

OPPOSITE, BOTTOM RIGHT

Cut-silk-velvet wall upholstery holds the Weimaraner-esque color of gray and reads like a luxe wood-grain texture.

ABOVE

From the chinoiserie fabric and silk lampshade to the sueded headboard, cotton bedskirt, and cashmere throw blanket, variations on a gray pepper this Leslie Cohen–designed bedroom.

There are myriad effective tools to create a nuanced room in gray scale:

- Play with the variations of tone in a strié paint finish, or a silk velvet that glows luminously with light and also holds deep saturated shadows.

- For a simple option, using five variations of a shade on an equal number of throw pillows.

- Drill down into the details and implement a few audacious touches to produce a memorable combination of still-subdued texture and tone. Gray can be boring when applied with a timid hand: If you render it in broad monotone strokes, you're dabbling with the dreary.

- Embrace age-enhancing patina: Think of how a color-enhanced black-and-white photo can look a little cheesy when contrasted with a faded original; or how wonderfully solemn Italian frescoes can suddenly appear almost garish when their tempering patinas are removed and the original gaudy coloration emerges again. Gray wash and varied tones add romance, so search out elements that look storied.

- Use gray as your main neutral, but add spark by pairing it with colors: Gray plays well with everything from cobalt blue to aqua, flax to taupe, lemon ice to sunflower yellow. Most people choose brown or beige as their predominant neutral, since wood plays a significant role in interior design, but gray is an inspired and exciting alternative, particularly if the rest of your palette tends toward cool—or if you're inclined to paint your wood white or ebonize it.

OPPOSITE
Layered shades of French gray (warmer and brown in tone) with accents of glass, metal, and black make for a very tailored and gender-neutral living room.

ABOVE RIGHT
Exposed concrete walls prove anything but plain.

BELOW RIGHT
A soft-gray wood armoire holds bed linens while a mirrored wall expands the room.

Design firm ODADA's exploration of living room as sculpture uses the cohesive effect of a soft gray scale as backdrop to a dramatic experiment. Sweeps of glossy white vinyl lie atop a plywood "over-floor" and rise onto and over the simple plywood furniture forms—coffee table, daybed, and chairs. Beneath them an exposed ebony floor serves up high contrast to highlight the beauty of negative space.

The gray values in each of these rooms
show how varied the take-away from
gray scale can be: These spaces run
the gamut, encapsulating traditional,
modern, warm, cold, masculine, and
feminine essences.

In this technically neutral dining room designed by Meg Braff, gray-patterned wallpaper, curtains with brush fringe, velvet seat backs with piping and tape trim detail, and leather seats create a great backdrop for a dinner party.

achieving the textured life

An intricate, multilayered effect doesn't happen overnight. It's not a one-dimensional "staged" look: It involves research, flexibility, and sophisticated decision-making over an evolving timeline. Think of compromise as your biggest asset, because it represents the point when you've lost control and must come up with solutions that take you out of your initial box.

In the interior design world, I tend to encounter two types of people: Those who constantly rethink themselves and start over, and those who begin with what they like and just keep going, working around mistakes rather than letting each misfire stop them cold, expanding their repertoire of design solutions and strategies. Those who keep starting over often end up with emotionally drained homes that look like incomplete pages in an interiors catalog. It's important to achieve a balance between respect for the process and a willingness to let the process evolve, and to evolve with it.

TAKE-OUT:

BLT BURGER 243-8826
GRADISCA 691-2683
CAFÉ ASEAN 633-0348
GREY DOG 462-0041
MURRAY'S 462-2830
WESTVILLE 741-7971

Chalkboard Paint

Chalkboard paint is exactly what its name suggests. Emulating a slate both in color and finish, it gives you walls you can write all over, then erase and chalk up again without fear of your paint burnishing away. I have such a wall in my bar/eat-in kitchen, since it's a great repository for kitchen scribbles, and the dark color hides my children's smeary handprints. Others use them to scrawl to-do lists, or to leave notes for house-guests. Plus, it washes down to a perfect, deep navy-gray.

mirrors and mirroring

Silver and other similar metallics are gray's more glamorous cousins. There's something primitively satisfying about mirrors. On their own, simply a glass with a frame around it, they serve as a curious, ornately bordered neutral element. But the second their surface carries a reflection, it mystically doubles a space or a face. The first known mirrors (not counting pools of water like the one Narcissus drowned in while admiring himself) were crafted not from glass, but from black obsidian and pieces of shale.

ABOVE

In Michael Bargo's small New York City apartment, mirrored doors conceal a kitchen's worth of storage.

RIGHT

An antiqued mirror has a dramatic, foggy quality in this dining room by Jan Showers. When spanning floor to ceiling, tiled squares make covering the expanse feasible and somehow soften the enormity of a huge sheet of glass.

An antique mirror in a narrow
entryway doubles the perception
of space and light.

REFLECTING LIFE

- Inset mirror into recessed paneled cabinetry in your master bathroom or bar.

- Place one at the end of a hallway to create the effect of an endless avenue.

- Mirrors are a designer's best tool when you want a room to glimmer with light and motion: Anything that moves in the room, moves in the mirror.

- In dark entryways, place a large mirror on a wall adjacent to a chandelier or sconce, so that you can easily amplify the light's effect.

- Antiqued mirror walls add old-world luminosity to a dining room.

- Hang your mirrors vertically to instantly lift your ceiling.

A mirrored surface is not only useful, it's also beautiful. Silver has a liquid quality that's incredibly calming and serene despite its hard veneer. In antique mirrors, age dulls the shine, softening and mottling the reflection in a much more livable way.

OPPOSITE, ABOVE LEFT
A classic, Louis Philippe style.

OPPOSITE, ABOVE RIGHT
A distressed frame against a cream wall presides over a simple white demi-lune table.

OPPOSITE, BELOW LEFT
A decorative element adds a high central focus point to a mirror.

OPPOSITE, BELOW RIGHT
Amy Lau used a green-lacquered buffet inset with reflective hammered-zinc panels, accented with chrome and old nickel on lamps and shades.

ABOVE
The pewterlike metallic leather on the dining settee dovetails with the mirror behind, the mercury glass lampshades above, and the warmth of the slightly reflective white and flax colored grass cloth walls in this dining nook.

ABOVE
Metals can be mixed, just as you'd mix time periods. Gary Spain uses brass sconces, antique bronze nailheads, and silvery beveled mirrors in this beautiful bedroom.

RIGHT
In my bedroom, the beveled glass top of a scallop-edged coffee table is reverse-painted in gold leaf and pairs wonderfully with an old silver ice bucket.

other glamorous metallics

Much as I've suggested you view natural materials such as jute, sisal, and linen, consider all metallics as neutrals in an otherwise black and white home, and employ them liberally.

I love mixing metals, both in my jewelry (after all, there are no hard-and-fast rules anymore for wearing gold and silver accessories together), and in my design schemes. Think about how timelessly lovely a gilt-edged mirror is, or how great a gold teapot or a set of bronze salt and pepper shakers looks against a mottled silver tray.

Whenever I start the selection process, I begin with a few good metallic antiques, since a shared wash of tarnish is the quickest and easiest way to unify a collection. Whether it's unlacquered brass or silver that has a Venetian, gold-speckled quality, these foundation pieces serve as the gracious hosts to a wide assemblage, welcoming even the most discordant elements into the space. In fact, I remember coming home once to the sad discovery that a very thoughtful houseguest had done me the "favor" of polishing my nicely aged, slightly dingy silver mint julep cups back into a flawless sparkle. They lost their soul for about six months, before regaining it through natural tarnish.

ABOVE RIGHT
Mixed metals, a silver lamp, and gilt frames are both simple and ornate.

RIGHT
Vessels of cut-glass crystal sparkle in a cluster.

ABOVE LEFT
What started as a problem of absentee moldings resolved itself thanks to silver metallic painted stripes that move from the walls to the ceiling and then out into a concentric squares pattern in this hyperglamorous powder room.

ABOVE RIGHT
Eddie Ross curates a beautiful deskscape with a vintage brass lamp and letter-writing tools.

RIGHT
Here, a gracious tufted sofa mixes comfortably with gold-legged, black glass–topped coffee tables.

OPPOSITE
Mirrored panels break up the black glossy walls and moldings and reflect views of Central Park South in panorama around the dining room.

black, white, and shots of color

The following section might seem a bit like cheating. But anyone who knows me at all is aware that I find color too consuming not to visit with it every once in a while. When it comes to actual, down-and-dirty living, it doesn't make any sense at all to let an overly rigid commitment to style limit the ease of your life. And truth be told, there are too many irresistibly great—and irrepressibly colorful—rooms out there that are more flexible palettewise, that were worth including. As you'll see, black and white make for a pretty spectacular backdrop.

Rooms are first and foremost for living–comfortably and well. If they can be beautiful 90 percent of the time, that's a wonderful thing. For that other 10 percent, get comfortable with a little bit of chaos. So let this be the 10 percent section where we enjoy the chaotic color layered in with our black and white. As the images in the following pages reveal, black and white allow the introduction of almost any conceivable color.

In the early years of mass paint production (back in the nineteenth century), black, yellow, and red were the primary colors in the palette (since they can all be sourced from naturally occurring pigments). Perhaps this is why rooms with these tones always look ageless and spot-on.

Cerulean blue becomes even more striking against curtain panels of a black-and-white cheetah pattern.

ABOVE LEFT

The intense symmetry of Philip
Gorrivan's living room is accented with
vibrant yellow and blue silk pillows.

ABOVE RIGHT

Matching lampshades, seat cushions,
and art make this room a three-beat
color story of black, white, and aqua.

RIGHT

Persimmon, cobalt, and cream
harmonize beautifully with black in
this Miles Redd dining room.

ABOVE LEFT
A pair of Warren Platner for Knoll chairs perch like yellow canaries beneath a black-and-white op-art piece.

ABOVE RIGHT
This highly polished black floor reflects and amplifies both the sun and the vigorously mod furniture shapes.

RIGHT
Red piano? Why not.

OPPOSITE
Harry Benson's photo of Mia Farrow and Frank Sinatra entering Truman Capote's Black and White Ball straddles a window in Eric Cohler's yellow, black, and white design.

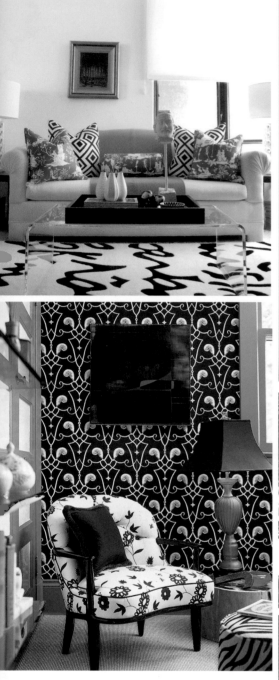

ABOVE AND TOP
A limited palette of black, white, and two accent colors allow myriad patterns to play in coordination: Caitlin Wilson accomplishes this through throw pillows and blankets, while Jay Jeffers plays up green-painted moldings.

OPPOSITE, ABOVE RIGHT AND BELOW RIGHT
In Lela Rose's living room and her son's bedroom, black, white, red, and yellow make a strong statement. In Benjamin Moore's early years (back in the nineteenth century), black, yellow, and red were the primary colors in their palette, since the colors could all be sourced from naturally occurring pigments.

ABOVE
Pamplemousse's design for a square entry space is centered on a brown, black, and white Ruhlmann circular rug and an ebony Jean Royère center table atop a reclaimed marble floor imported from France. Bold pops of red and yellow from Fridel Dzubas's *Kronion* painting on one of the walls break up the color scheme.

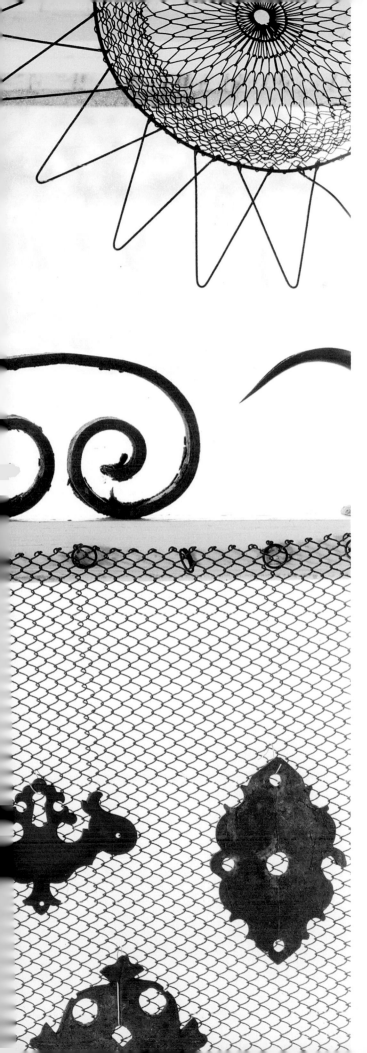

7 THE ART OF COLLECTING

using minor moments to make major statements

"If you have it, display it."

—Carleton Varney

ANYONE WHO HAS SPENT TIME at an antiques mall or a flea market has seen firsthand the particular pull of collecting. There's a lot of random stuff in this world, and figuring out what you love enough to hunt for brings order—and purpose—not only to these shopping missions, but to your aesthetic in general. Whether you choose to use the cohesiveness of black and white as a means to refine your treasure-hunting expeditions (the colors can homogenize even the most random assortment), or whether you use your collections to add splashes of color to a room that's an otherwise black and white canvas, it is these celebrated groupings that prove most expressive.

Small touches—bud vases on the bedside table, the silver picture frames on the dresser, or, in my house, vintage paper party hats, placed in shadow boxes and hung—are not only emblematic of an underlying sensibility, they're generally deeply personal. Why does one person choose Pez dispensers while another traffics in enameled pillboxes?

Collections have impact that solitary objects don't. A wall of books in a library looks much more striking than a handful of them stacked on a lone shelf. And when you winnow some collections to a single color, you will find they turn meaningful and evocative, because the various forms come to the forefront, emphasizing what made the objects worthy of notice in the first place.

Clearly, some collections benefit from a wealth of different colors—Matchbox cars, toy soldiers, handblown ashtrays . . . but when the collection strays from a very specific type and shape, the restraint of black and white can turn what is otherwise clutter into something with a clear and defined thesis. A collection of animal figurines, of all different scales and craft levels, looks like a family when each is cast from crisp white bisque; black vases—some urnlike, others for little bud blossoms—would be entirely unremarkable alone, but when grouped, they become a decisive statement.

This collection of Bialetti espresso
makers sees real action day to day in
Rita Konig's kitchen.

OPPOSITE

Even atop a low black coffee table, spindly black Dansk candlesticks look striking with their upward reach.

ABOVE LEFT

Black ebony wood containers rest on a dressing table.

ABOVE RIGHT

As long as they speak to days of faded glory, trophies won't smack of bravado and show-offyness. A collection of old ones can be sweet, as displayed by Thomas Smythe on an étagère.

BELOW RIGHT

Symmetrically arranged mounted antlers create an orderly wallpaper-like effect while a painted zigzag pattern runs jaggedly across the floor in the Haus Interior store.

ABOVE LEFT
A lone black Nymphenburg elephant
sits on a glossy lacquered table.

RIGHT
Black transfer ware plates dress a white
painted beadboard cupboard.

finding the amazing and unexpected item to collect

Whether you have a predilection for antique irons, Art Deco cigarette cases, or Herend figurines, there are plenty of contenders for your collection. It takes a certain amount of time and experience to know what's rare and what's not, and what an item is theoretically worth. Until you really know what you're doing, don't get too wrapped up in the minutiae. You're going to make some mistakes, and either overpay or amass pieces you later realize you don't love. Don't worry; this is the price of knowledge. It's a far better alternative than walking away from something that you know in your heart you must have, especially when it could also be one of a kind.

Here's how to make an informed decision:

- While you're building your mental encyclopedia of all things collectible, walk the markets and antiques malls just to see what's out there; you'll be amazed at what you find, whether it's taxidermied swans, Rotary Club drink stirrers, 1960s porn, or the odd totem pole.

- Cross-reference your field studies with eBay, just to be sure that everything is lining up (for more on online auctions, see page 179). You can start with common, everyday items, like white vases or silver animal figurines, or you can pursue something obscure and hard to find, like black steel lace from Berlin in Napoleonic times. Start wandering to see what sparks your imagination—you'll know just the thing to set you off when you find it.

- I generally steer clear of anything that's too expensive, because that involves an extra level of authority or a beefy budget. I also don't want to have to stress over the authenticity (or lack thereof) of diamonds while hovering over a table of estate jewelry in a mud-filled field, delirious with flea rapture and dangerously overcaffeinated.

A mixture of black and white objects, notebooks, and vases fill a black bookshelf.

ABOVE LEFT
An assemblage of machinist parts.

ABOVE RIGHT
Grouped pound ridge pottery.

RIGHT
Nothing highlights a collection more than architectural forethought. Here an arched niche is filled with branchlike plaster brackets holding a collection of vases in Axel Vervoordt's dining room.

OPPOSITE, TOP
Maybe it's my Palm Beach heritage, but I'll always have a soft spot for sailor's valentines, so named because sailors used to assemble them on the sea for loved ones, using the only supplies around. Marion McEvoy's white shells set in ebony frames adhere to a theme of dramatic black bordering throughout her house.

OPPOSITE, BOTTOM
Nautical meets geographic in this stunning collection of ivory, leather, rope, and bone objects.

Searching and Shopping eBay

1 Set your preferences to search for key words of particular interest to you (say, Vaseline glass, match strikes, or chinoiserie); the more specific the better.

2 Once you get in the collecting mind-set, you're going to happen on plenty of things you'll want to buy. I make it my practice to bid once at my maximum, somewhat close to the auction's end (they'll send you an alert if you request it), and walk away.

3 Being fatalistic about the process generally works out, because invariably, another version of the same thing—or occasionally, something you like even more than the original—will eventually make its way onto the site, and into your hands. If it's meant to be, it will be.

4 Photos can be deceiving. Always remember to check dimensions before purchasing.

5 And a final word of warning: Check the shipping charges before you bid!

COLLECTING FOR MINIMALISTS

TOP
A tiny 1″ tall intaglio, when framed with oversize mat, can grow to a dramatic 36″ tall framed piece.

ABOVE
A bunching of whisks and other utensils exposed on a kitchen counter takes on utilitarian sculptural significance.

ABOVE RIGHT
Boxes and vintage seltzer bottles are tidily arranged over a buffet covered in other beautifully grouped objects and florists' buckets.

There are many people who aren't collectors at all, who deem any unnecessary item a tchotchke, or just another surface that requires dusting. If you are a minimalist like this, enrich a room with a large, meaningful item—a huge painting, a significant piece of furniture—that won't require shelf space and can fill a wall.

1 Consider collecting containers—if you hate the bric-a-brac of life, look for items in which you can conceal it all, like stainless-steel bread boxes, simple apothecary jars, or white ceramic bins.

2 Use all the money you've saved on theoretically useless clutter to invest in an important painting or photograph.

3 Only collect elements that have a legitimate purpose.

4 Collect items that live in albums, like ornithological prints and rare stamps.

A cluster of framed vintage medical splints hangs over the elongated horizontal lines of a mid-century four-drawer console table.

PRECEDING PAGES
Open shelving frames the entry into a rustic dining room. A collection of glass decanters and bottles spills from one room to the next by maintaining the same height.

ABOVE
Camera equipment, film reels, and black metal housings draw the eye up to the top shelf, which runs around the perimeter of this study.

RIGHT
Built-in bookshelves stand almost naked of literature, filled instead with black urns, busts, and objects.

COLLECTING FOR MAXIMALISTS

Clearly, nobody wants his or her house to look like an episode of *Hoarders,* so there are a few foolproof ways for maximalists to keep the collecting fairly organized.

1   Each piece doesn't need to be surrounded by empty, clarifying space, but you need some areas of relief. Congregate your groupings and leave significant spots clutter-free (half of the coffee table, an entire side table).

2   Move your collections to the wall: Think of the Pitti Palace in Florence, where paintings literally cover the walls from floor to ceiling and no space is unfilled. If that concept enchants you, approach your walls with equal gusto, and let the synergy of the grouping you assemble produce an extraordinary effect. Imagine how striking an expanse of black-and-white photographs might look, whether they're vintage panoramas of sports teams and military academies or Edward Curtis portraits.

3   If you're feeling a little more adventurous, make a wall of many shapes, media, and periods, mixing tiny oil paintings with needlepoint tapestries and Chinese plates.

4   Edit like crazy. You don't need to display everything at once. It's also wise to cap off a collection and decide that you will allow no more than ten or fifteen of any single item.

5   Play with scale: Counter a collection of large elements, like taxidermy or trophies, with something in miniature, such as thimbles or tiny glass figurines.

ABOVE RIGHT

A Chinese cabinet houses jewelry and stands humbly beneath a collection of beaded necklaces that have broken free of their drawers.

RIGHT

A flock of white birds rests on a ledge high above this entry.

hanging collections

A piece of art that is major both in scale and in quality is required to anchor an entire wall. Though I've seen exquisite, exceptionally small paintings hold the fort on occasion (if only because, as you press your nose to see it, the teeny-tiny brushstrokes are awe-inspiring), single smallish items generally look lonely in a great expanse. So don't leave an individual piece to languish on its own! Just as a memorable dinner party generally requires more than *one* voluble guest, a wall needs a number of good pieces that can converse well with one another.

RIGHT
Small images framed on white matting stand out against a black wall and black-painted door in a Libby Cameron–designed room. The arrangement seems engaged in a conversation, each frame working in relationship to another.

OPPOSITE
A huge image of marblelike feet seemingly step across the upholstery, making a towering but still barefoot and humanizing centerpiece in this living room.

THE ORDERLY, PRECISE HANG

1   If this is your preference, you're going to want to hang artwork, such as black-and-white photographs, that are uniform in both size and frame and composed in a perfect grid.

2   Complete your collection before you hang a single thing: You will want the elements to be centered and immutable.

3   Unless you're handy with a level and a measuring tape, bring in a professional for this job: If any of the pictures are even slightly off-kilter, the effect will be unsettling, since you desire symmetry and balance in the first place. Using two hanging points on smaller pieces may seem unnecessary, but they will shift less.

4   True perfectionists and DIY-ers should consider tracing the shape of their pieces onto butcher's paper, marking where the hooks catch when there's weight on the wire, and taping the paper to the wall—a nail will go right through it at the correct point, and then you can tear it down once the art is up. For a look of organized chaos, use painter's tape to mark a big rectangle on your wall. Line the edges of your art along the tape on all sides and vary the placement in the middle.

OPPOSITE

An arrangement of vertical wood-framed mirrors in antique dealers Angus Wilke and Len Morgan's house elevates the height of the room as flashes of reflected light climb the wall.

BELOW LEFT

A set of cow prints is pleasingly homogenous as they all stare in the same direction.

BELOW RIGHT

Even though the pieces vary in size, all the outer borders line up to create one large rectangle, adding up to a highly precise and edited grouping.

THE ORGANIC, UNFETTERED HANG

ABOVE

In this Windsor Smith–designed stairwell, white-framed photography radiates out from the central, larger, and darker photograph.

OPPOSITE

I've had this photo hung above my desk for inspiration for years. In a bedroom by designer Nannette Brown, black-framed portraits rise to the top of a pitched ceiling over an ebonized turned wooden bed.

1   Let your display be willy-nilly. I hang the centerpiece, or largest piece, first, and then the others, slowly radiating out—eyeballing the overall look and feel as I go.

2   If filling a wall, make sure you've gathered a critical mass of items before you begin. The wall doesn't have to be full at the outset (leave room to grow!), but it should look finished in concept as it evolves. Given a lot of art, even the most impulsive art hangers should rein themselves in and arrange all the pieces on the floor before they install the first picture hanger.

3   Remember, the wall can wear more than flat framed art. Think three-dimensional and add brackets, candle sconces, plates, and hangable objects.

collecting while you travel: amazing arts and crafts from around the world

I'm grappling with issues of collecting fixation firsthand, ever since my husband surprised me with an onset of samurai obsession. Our living room and minimal storage space have been peopled with an ever-growing cast of fancily dressed tiny warriors. I'm getting increasingly desperate for something small and inexpensive to replace his yen for samurai!

If there's a market, souk, or bazaar in close proximity to my travel destination, all plans of carry-on baggage are certifiably doomed (I've been known to leave the contents of my suitcase behind in favor of loot). As happens to many travelers, I can get so swept up in a country's cultural and aesthetic sensibility that I completely forget the realities of my design scheme back home, and will end up buying, say, twenty ikats, because I can't bear to leave them behind. Here are a few of the ways I repurpose these finds:

1   I often relinquish a few chosen items to good friends as birthday gifts, understanding that they may have rooms that are more accommodating of wildly exotic touches.

2   I create collections in transit and buy in bulk: If I have to have a beaded animal, I trust that it will only hold its place if it's in the company of two others. Otherwise it will look lonely and random, unless it works in a specific color scheme I've created or is large in scale.

3   I lose all sense of what's a reasonable amount to pay when I encounter great woven fabrics on the road, but it's easy to turn these into throw pillows or scarves, giving them justifiable use!

Much of what I've found has been magically colorful, like the embroidery from the Hmong villagers in Laos, or the traditional khangas of Kenya, but there are wonderful black and white objects, too, such as vases in geometric designs from Peru, handwoven baskets from Uganda, Gansey sweaters from Ireland, Belgian lace, Batik prints from Bali, or lacquerware from Burma.

The Art of Decluttering

Invariably, you're going to purchase things over the years that you later decide you can live without. These items should not litter your shelves.

- Decluttering is absolutely necessary every six months, right before the holiday season takes off, and then again before it gets warm.

- I like to rotate my accessories—or at least rearrange them—just to mix it up and refresh the room. Your eyes will adjust to your interior landscapes and begin to jump over things that become too familiar. Putting them in a new context breathes new life into them.

- The most expedient approach is to corral everything from your shelves into an area where you can dust it all and reassess, before restyling your entire house or room.

- If you're on the fence about whether something should stay or go, relegate it to a closet or a drawer and see if you even notice it's gone. Three months later, pay it a visit and you'll know instantly whether it's been missed or whether you feel more disconnected. The intermediate step always eases the breakup!

Unifying Washes of Paint or Paper

Just as ebonizing a floor and staining furniture can unify an entire room, a trusty can of spray paint or a roll of wallpaper can unify a collection. This technique works well if you're more interested in the form of the objects than their color, if you're having a hard time making a group of pieces work together, and especially if the items aren't valuable. Take a shot of gold or white spray paint to an array of 1960s plastic animal figurines to make them worthy of your child's bedroom, or wrap a handful of ugly hardcovers with gorgeous William Morris wallpaper for a small bookshelf in the entryway.

8 IMPORTANT DETAILS AND ENTERTAINING using black and white as a centerpiece

"Have nothing in your houses which you do not know to be useful or believe to be beautiful."

—William Morris

THIS CHAPTER EXPLORES all sorts of immediate and easy access points for sprinkling a little black-and-white stardust into your life; from simple floral centerpieces in inventive silver julep cups, to that one major item that's going to make the entire room. Harnessing the power of black and white doesn't need to be an exhaustive, all-encompassing undertaking. You can also treat it as the spice that will make your rooms and events more piquant, nuanced, and rich.

Come dinnertime, I'm usually wrestling with one of two approaches to the menu when I'm cooking: I'm either following a recipe and crossing my fingers that I can pull off a complicated, highly seasoned dish loaded with potentially competing flavors, or I'm playing it safer, building my meal around one basic, excellent, underlying ingredient that I regard as a "sure thing," like sautéed soft-shell crabs, or a leg of New Zealand lamb—plus a dash of salt and pepper. Putting together a great room is much like preparing a great meal. You can go for it, having faith that with tinkering and patience you can deliver something memorable and one-of-a-kind, or you can focus your energies on one central item that you know will produce reliable, impressive results. We've discussed the first approach at length in this book, since my general M.O. is to spread multiple striking pieces across a space, but it's important to delve into the merits of the second strategy as well.

PRECEDING PAGES
Eddie Ross's collection of vintage tableware frames a handsome buffet, where tea and cupcakes await the party.

ABOVE
A black and gilt chinoiserie corner cabinet sings the low notes behind the willowy voice of a curvaceous white-framed chair.

Black and white tent-striped fabric
dresses up a pair of black-framed
chairs.

choosing your soloist

ABOVE

This spiderlike lamp spans over the
dining table, seemingly responsible for
the strong vertical lines of black tape
trim in the windows and the stripes of
the wallpaper.

OPPOSITE

The intense graphic pattern of the
art centered over the tufted sofa is
grounded by the dark framing of black
doors, pillows, and a pair of chairs in
Carole Katleman and Daniel Cuevas's
living room design.

If a room is to hinge on one attention-getting object, you need to make sure that this foundation piece deserves the spotlight it will command. I call these pieces "soloists" because they stand out from the rest, even though they must harmonize with the other elements in the room; and the elements you have chosen to play backup need to support the soloist, of course. Find pieces that bolster and flatter your main attraction, rather than pieces that might compete with it or undermine the power of your star performer.

Finding the ideal centerpiece doesn't have to involve a major investment in a historically significant item. Consider transforming something everyday into something extraordinary. Lacquer a ho-hum bistro table. Paint a bamboo screen glossy black and convert it into a headboard. Use a white garden trellis on a wall instead of wallpaper.

You can also introduce single shots of black and white into a room as lowlights and highlights: Just as color pops even more against a black and white backdrop, black and white extras add complexity to a color-saturated world. Try hanging a distinctive, jet-toned chandelier over your dining table for dark luster, or placing milk glass lamps on bedside tables.

OPPOSITE
Nannette Brown hangs a humble bronze chandelier, which draws the eye up from the heft of a black-painted fireplace.

LEFT
Laurann Claridge ingeniously employs a gothic-arch-shaped folding screen as a headboard.

ABOVE
An authoritative-looking portrait hangs over a black-striéd marble fireplace in Michael Bargo's studio.

ABOVE LEFT
Custom-embroidered towels add a posh factor to black and white checkered bathroom floors.

ABOVE RIGHT
A decoupaged wall in John Derian's home assumes a patchwork effect thanks to alabaster and ink-typeset book pages.

BELOW LEFT AND RIGHT
Brightly colored chandeliers capture the spotlight while black paint unifies a charming hodgepodge of chair shapes in these two dining rooms.

subtle tweaking for big rewards

While the pervasive—and blessedly easy—approach to shopping in this country is to buy clothes off the rack and wear them right out of the store, tailoring shows assets to greater advantage and minimizes flaws.

Generally, most home furnishings come in standard shapes and sizes that require no modifications. Why would you want to tinker with the length or width of a bed, for example, when you'd never be able to find sheets that fit it? But if you have a plain four-poster bed frame, why not paint it with a Fornasetti-like black and white pattern, and boost your luxe level? A Biedermeier sofa can become a showpiece if you upholster it in daring fabric; a negligible transom window can be upgraded with an installment of leaded glass. There are occasions in every room where subtle tailoring can make a piece look altogether better, and lend your space more character and refinement.

You can modify everyday things in small ways, too, such as by decoupaging a small table or a handful of terra-cotta pots with pages from old books, and then grouping them on a shelf. I've seen stunning centerpieces crafted from Lombok shells and air plants, and old advertising signs turned into a coffee table. Don't think of the items you bring into your home as inviolate, finished things—minor or major modifications can make a piece even more your own.

ABOVE RIGHT
Rita Konig's lampshade has a delightful diagonal gray trim treatment. She enlivens a black side table with a piece of blue mirrored glass.

RIGHT
Eddie Ross found vintage marbled paper and had lamp shades custom made for these vintage black glass lamps in his Milford, New York, living room.

entertaining in black and white

There's something august, something striking, something *significant* about emphasizing black and white, something that says, "Take notice; remember this occasion." While this can be invoked through interior design choices, entertaining in this palette has a particularly powerful aura. There's a tradition of people making extraordinary efforts with black and white celebrations. Truman Capote's famous Black and White Ball is often called "the party of the century." At debutante balls, young women dress in white to mark the assumption of their traditional role in the human drama, a new generation coming of age. Even today, at chic Chanel parties, ingénues, movie stars, celebrities, and bigwigs dress like elegant goths, deploying the sophistication of Coco Chanel's favored black and white palette. A black and white place setting—or even an all-white place setting in pristine porcelain—dresses up the simplest menu.

Whether for a dinner party for six or an anniversary party for one hundred, a simplified color palette can reduce prep time, unify a scheme, and magnify the effect you hope to create. When you can't pick from the whole array of flowers at your local deli, and must limit yourself to white and green instead, the arrangement has to compensate with its simplicity and elegance. A profusion of ranunculus and poppies and peonies may be lovely; but tall, slender, white chrysanthemums with their spiky poufs, scepterlike stalks of irises, the delicate spread of Queen Anne's lace, or even branches of white cherry blossoms make a strong, expressive statement. The same goes for platters, cocktail napkins, and the pieces with which you dress the table. It may sound daunting to limit yourself from the outset, but it will help refine the decision-making process, and may ultimately leave you more time to get ready yourself!

table settings

ABOVE LEFT

Timothy Whealon sets a tiny table in front of a built-in banquette for holding drinks and snacks.

ABOVE RIGHT

For an open-air country-house dinner, Eddie Ross splatter-painted a tablecloth for an unexpected splash of whimsy.

BELOW RIGHT

All-white china settings can look humble and casual for everyday use, but they still rise easily to more formal occasions.

OPPOSITE

The upturned white-glass leaves of a Murano chandelier hover over a dinner setting of clear-glass plates atop gray trellis and glass-topped place mats. Guests may see through to—but not necessarily feel—the rough-hewn gray and apricot sandstone table beneath.

easy, stunning floral arrangements

A white tablecloth casually graces the
top of a Swedish white dining room.

I prefer flower arrangements that consist of a mass of a single variety of flower. Pink dahlias, hydrangeas, purple-throated calla lilies, white carnations, and white dahlias bring petaled delicacy into each of these rooms.

Entertaining Cheat Sheet

- Do your math: If it's a cocktail party, overbuy on the liquor so you're not forced to run out for more halfway through.

- I like humble, indulgent food for parties, rather than fussy, overly intricate appetizers. Taste should be paramount: I've never known anyone to turn down an abundant selection of cheeses, or figs wrapped in prosciutto, particularly when they're prettily arranged.

- Keep the hors d'oeuvres bite-size: Managing a drink, a plate, and a fork and knife while standing is uncomfortable and unwieldy.

- If at all possible, provide real glassware, plates, and cocktail napkins—besides being kinder to the environment, it's much more elegant. I have a huge collection of inexpensive stacking glass tumblers from CB2 that are super handy for last-minute parties.

- Collect bud vases for miniature flower arrangements. Place a small arrangement above each knife. It's much less invasive than giant bouquets in the middle of the table, and it spreads the prettiness around.

- If it's a seated dinner and there's space on the table or at a buffet area, I like to let guests serve themselves, rather than plating the food in the kitchen. It makes the dinner more convivial, plus I hate forcing things that might not be to someone's taste to sit on the plate taunting them all night.

- While most of the food should be congregated on one, central table, scatter bowls of nuts and treats around the party.

- Hire a bartender (look to a local college if you don't know one) to pour and pass drinks, and tidy up after guests. People tend to lose track of their glasses and plates, and will invariably just take a new one rather than risk taking someone else's.

- The food should be cleared away about an hour before you want the event to wrap up.

- For everyday, snap up an antique bar cart with all the fixings: It makes even the mixing of a drink seem ceremonial.

9 HARD-WORKING SPACES
black and white bathrooms and kitchens

"Be marble to his soot, and to his black be white."

—W. H. Auden

IF YOUR BUDGET ALLOWS, splash out on your bathrooms, kitchen, and entryway. Make these spaces lavish, inviting, and comfortable. As the most utilitarian spaces in your home, they are, by definition, the most *used* places. For that reason, and because it is very expensive to revise a kitchen later, they deserve the greatest consideration. The purposes of these rooms dictate most of the furnishings that fill them, so it's best to let the basic elements—walls, floors, countertops, and color—shape the aesthetic statement.

Hard-wearing, durable, and easy to clean, black and white is also a great shortcut to creating a mood in places that don't always allow room for lots of atmosphere-establishing "extras." The energy and effectiveness of your concept absolutely depends on the quality of the materials you choose, and the execution of their design.

In your bathroom, would you like the tile to be handmade, with varied edges and imperfections that a shiny glaze will emphasize, or do you want machine-cut matte tiles in a graphic brick design? And in your kitchen, will your cabinets have a glossy lacquer finish or should they be hand-painted, so brush marks show through? As minor and finicky as these decisions may seem, they make the difference between a room that gives off a cozy, country-house feel and one that projects a contemporary urbane mood. Which aura do you want around you?

PRECEDING PAGES
Glass-faced cabinets, brass-accented hardware, and strong lighting subtly contradict the rough nature of a wood plank island in Wende Cohen's kitchen design.

ABOVE
Thomas Smythe used black lower cabinets and dark stone floors as an anchor to light-painted cabinet uppers.

In my Carrara marble bathroom, a dark gray bardiglio and white Thassos basketwave marble pattern moves diagonally across the floor, while ebonized wood frames the mirrors and cabinets.

black, gray, and white bathrooms

Color contrast is never starker than in bathrooms, where porcelain plumbing fixtures set the tone. They're generally an ultra-bright shade of white; so when you choose paint, wallpaper, or flooring, consider how they will coordinate. This is a lesson that's not worth learning the hard way. If your tile work or paint doesn't match the porcelain fixtures, your additional bathroom elements will stand out in ungainly contrast. No amount of scrubbing can make a gray look white next to the absolute white of porcelain. Here are a few favorite examples of washrooms in our preferred palette.

Apothecary-Like Bathroom Setups

If you're anything like me, you're probably more curious about what's *on* the shelves of your friends' bathrooms than about what those shelves are made of. I believe this stems from the intimacy of personal choice—in the most intimate of spaces. I'm sometimes a loyalist to beauty product packaging more so than I am to the actual product. My bathrooms bulge with gorgeously papered scented soaps I'm loath to unwrap; with soldier-like ranks of Jo Malone's heavenly scented perfumes and bath oils; even with tiny Chanel-logo'd bottles lined up like a toe nail polish arsenal. I am especially vulnerable to excess purchasing of Chanel, YSL, Givenchy, and Nars makeup because I love how their sophisticated black and gold cases look en masse. (I loathe logos on almost anything else, so I attribute it to appealing product design more than luxury brand worship.)

It may often look like I don't own a hairbrush, but I'm rarely without a Mason Pearson brush. Clean white powder puffs and Q-tips have the same irresistible effect on me. The tools of beauty should be as beautiful to look at as the end result.

Through a gothic arched doorway, the reflection of vintage apothecary bottles is caught in a vanity mirror.

kitchens to live in

In addition to the choice of materials, the floorplan is the other top consideration when creating or renovating a kitchen. Whether or not square footage is a prime concern in your kitchen design, there's a logical place where the trash compactor should go; a right spot for a built-in mission-control desk; a prime location for a kitchen island. Whether DIY-ing the job or working with an architect, tape out kitchen plans on the floor, and then test-drive the plan by moving around it as if preparing a meal. Everything should feel instinctual and intuitive, particularly since there are dangerous factors at play—fire and water, ovens and burners, sinks, spills and slips . . . and little hands that swing fridge doors open just as you're to ferrying the boiling pot of pasta to the sink.

ABOVE

Whether you are the one cooking or waiting to be passed eggs your style, there is nothing that makes a kitchen more cozy than some upholstery. A banquette offers maximum seating and the excuse for soft throw pillows. Here Christina Murphy creates the perfect setting to sip and sun kitchenside.

RIGHT

Colorful dish towels are an easy way to add temporary color to a classic kitchen. Meanwhile, fresh flowers, a bowl of fruit, and fun accessories can change the entire mood without resorting to swapping out tile or wallpaper.

Industrial fishermen's lamps hang in
this pristine white kitchen. Rolling pins
make for a charming collection on the
walls.

ABOVE
Large slabs of paneled Carrara marble make a most impressive kitchen island with a stunning, rough-hewn floor.

OPPOSITE, TOP
The abundant use of stainless steel and brass make this kitchen a glimmering masterpiece.

OPPOSITE, BOTTOM
Simple cream cabinets play off penny-dot backsplashes made from an irregular and hand-mixed selection of tiles chosen in the palest of cupcake icing colors.

the best black
and white tile,
slab, and brick
options

WHITE AND GRAY SPECTRUM MARBLE: THASSOS, CARRARA, CALACATTA, and STATUARY Michelangelo carved only in white marble, most of it excavated from the quarries of Carrara, Italy. These days, Carrara-style marble is known for its gray-veined tones and is mined in many places, making it inexpensive and immensely popular.

Despite its beauty and its hardness, marble is deceptively fragile. It's not impervious to heat, and it's very susceptible to acidic liquids; it can stain or scratch. If you prefer a highly polished finish and are able to continually re-seal the slabs, your marble can last for a long time. If you want the pure white of Thassos (the most stain prone) but don't want the maintenance trouble, the same look can be achieved with composite white glass.

BLACK MARBLE: NERO, PORTORO, ST. LAURANT There's something Jazz Age, grand, and opulent about black Portoro marble (a misnomer, as it's actually a kind of limestone). Dark as ebony, it is often streaked with a fretwork of golden veining, like tendrils of amber seaweed trailing through dark water. Portoro and St. Laurant (a similar but less expensive option) are experiencing a revival lately. Nero is a less expensive and more consistently black marble, though it does have frequent white veins.

GRANITE Granite can handle high temperatures and hard use, making it one of the most trusted kitchen and floor materials on the market. Still, I find most versions of it a bit too chunky, and too sugary and sparkly in texture when polished. I prefer honed or fired granites to avoid those aesthetic drawbacks. In black granite, though, they are almost nonexistent, which I think makes it a spectacularly versatile material.

QUARTZ Entire buildings are crafted from quartz, which is the second most common mineral on earth (after feldspar). Quartz comes in many colors, varieties, and transparency levels (including as a semiprecious stone) and can be used for slabs, tiles, and even floors. When we use it for countertops, it is usually a very durable engineered composite like Ceasarstone or Silestone.

SOAPSTONE As its name suggests, soapstone, which is naturally gray, has the soft feel of soap. It has a high proportion of talc, and has been used for carving for thousands of years. It's great for hearths (it evenly distributes heat), counters (it gets great patina over time), and steps (it's weather-resistant).

SLATE Formerly used for blackboards, slate is essentially a compacted blend of clay and shale. Due to its rocky composition, it has an inconsistent, bumpy surface. It's heat- and scratch-resistant, making it a sturdy choice for counters, floors, and fireplaces.

LIMESTONE Limestone resembles rock in its quality, durability, and accessibility (it makes up about 10 percent of all sedimentary stone). It's good for paving, floors, countertops, and outdoor pathways, but the lighter colors can discolor very easily, so make sure to seal it well and frequently. Bluestone, when waxed, is a beautiful "amost black." I have used it many times as cabochons in large fields of cream limestone. It makes a magnificent tabletop as well.

TRAVERTINE In the limestone family, travertine is often white or cream in color, and can be cut so thin it looks almost translucent.

SANDSTONE Available in gray, white, and black (along with a roster of other colors), sandstone is easily cut and carved. Similar to limestone because it is highly stainable, it is otherwise more durable and used frequently outdoors.

PORCELAIN Dense and smooth with a uniform face, porcelain tiles are made from compressed ceramic dust. The upside of a matte, or unglazed, finish is that chips aren't visible since the material is consistent throughout. A highly polished finish is ideal for bathroom walls, though it can get slick when used on the floor in large pieces.

GLASS Colored tiles or reverse-painted larger pieces make beautiful semi-reflective backsplashes or high-gloss walls.

Bathrooms can be defined by a smorgasbord of different materials and layouts. Consider straight lays, pinwheels, herringbone, diagonal herringbone, brick set, offset stagger, Versailles, Windmill, basketweave, and plaid . . . to list just a small sampling.

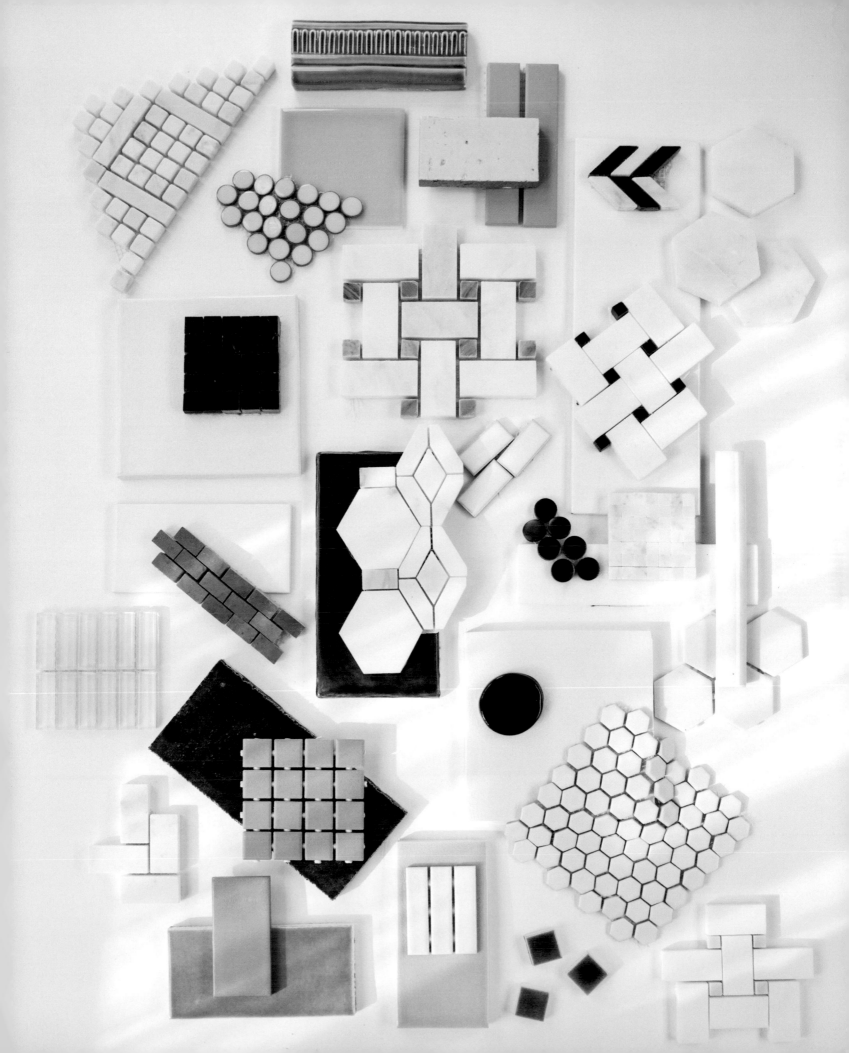

10 CLEANEST QUALITIES
keeping your whites white, and your blacks black

"What is elegance? Soap and water!"

—Cecil Beaton

"All of us have moments in our lives that test our courage. Taking children into a house with white carpet is one of them."

—Erma Bombeck

WHITE LAB COATS were initially dreamed up for doctors and scientists not only because they give an effect of brightness and purity, but because they reveal contamination. This was useful and reassuring in fields in which cleanliness was critical to health and accurate results. But it also meant that one stain would destroy a lab coat's spotless effect.

Many of my clients balk at the idea of a white couch, immediately picturing marks and spots, telling themselves they can't keep it clean, and fearing that it will quickly deteriorate into something much grubbier than the pristine object they were introduced to. But the reality is that a white couch, if slip-covered, can stay white for decades, so long as you don't aggressively grind your muddy shoes into it. White towels and sheets can be laundered at extremely high temperatures. Plus, there's bleach. That's why the nation's most successful high-end hotel chains so often use white linens: They wear well and are easy to care for, despite a fairly steady stream of traffic.

There's no need to chase after your children and houseguests with premoistened paper towels, or to keep your sofas protected with sheets. What is the point of furniture that you can't use? I tend to breathe a deep sigh of relief as soon as something "new" is baptized with a (hopefully small) stain. And in general, I just try to stay a few feet ahead of the mess, which is why this chapter is packed with easy cleaning tips and tricks for keeping it all in hand.

ABOVE LEFT
A pair of white upholstered sofas rest brightly on a dark-stained floor, kissed ever so slightly by the break of white curtain panels.

LEFT
A smocking detail from a curtain header can be dusted with a hairdryer.

the cleanliness paradox

BELOW
Stone floors are easily sweepable, but you have to be careful not to smudge white walls in the process. Keep touch-up paint handy for rooms where there are no base moldings.

OPPOSITE, LEFT
Silver-leaf tiles reflect light, and their subtle mottling conveniently hide watermarks.

Upkeep is sometimes counterintuitive. A black couch can easily handle some insults that a white couch doesn't take in stride—like Magic Marker and red wine—but it is not necessarily superior to a white couch in hiding dirt. In fact, dark surfaces reveal every speck of dust and every strand of dog hair, requiring fairly constant dusting.

Nature's Paradox

Who would imagine that a destructive, raging forest fire is actually essential to a forest's long-term health and growth? Its purifying effect is a total conundrum. Not only can charcoal filter water, but in the olden days, pioneer women used ash to launder clothing, turning the ash into lye, then mixing it with fat to make soap.

the bottom line:
black and white keep you honest

Just because dirt and dust are omnipresent doesn't mean that we have to let them dominate the color schemes of our lives. Black and white bathrooms combine the cleaning challenges and advantages of both colors, which is probably one of the reasons why they are so popular and classic. A black and white palette keeps you honest because it accentuates dirt, giving you visible reminders that it's time to pick up the scrub brush—reminders you wouldn't get in a taupe and greige world. Even if you're not seeing it, the dirt and grime are there, camouflaged in an oatmeal-colored carpet. I'd much rather see what I'm up against!

BELOW CENTER
The nickel legs and fixtures in this spotless, marble-clad bathroom sparkle.

BELOW RIGHT
Black-paneled walls and a free-standing porcelain tub make for a dramatic bathroom—and hide the rigors of everyday use.

cleaning upholstery

A powerful vacuum cleaner is one of the more underrated tools in the effective cleaner's arsenal. Remember that it's not intended just for floors. When it comes to shelving, the vacuum is a far more effective duster than a wad of paper towels or a cloth (these scatter just as much dust as they collect, and getting them wet with cleaner creates a dangerous sludge). As a bonus, the vacuum is much more eco-friendly.

MAXIMIZE ATTACHMENTS More important, vacuums come with an ever-handy, often overlooked upholstery attachment. This should be your first line of defense when it comes to couches, curtains, and even lampshades, since it lifts specks out of the cloth without grinding them in. While most slipcovers can be either laundered or dry-cleaned (read tags carefully first), they're liable to shrink and wrinkle, so use these methods as a very last resort.

SPOT-CLEANING METHODS When stains happen—which they invariably will—try to gently spot clean. Be sure that you're not working with a dry-clean-only fabric first, and if you're unsure, test your mixture on a piece of fabric that isn't visible (i.e., the underside of a cushion or back side of a skirt). Dissolve a small amount of dishwashing detergent in water (1:4 ratio), mix well, and then rub it in with a softly bristled brush. After the mark is lifted, use a lightly moistened washcloth to remove any residue.

REMOVING PET HAIR If your pets shed a lot, put your hand in a rubber dishwashing glove and swipe it gently across anything upholstered—it acts as a veritable magnet for all that unwanted hair. A Gonzo sponge works the same magic on almost any surface, as do lint rollers, though they aren't as environmentally sound.

Slipcovers on white linen dining chairs make them more stain-averse than you might think!

cleaning leather

There are a few gentle, tried-and-true methods for cleaning leather. I like good old-fashioned saddle soap, since it conditions as it cleans. Essentially, you're going to create a lather using a moistened cloth, and then buff the leather well. If you're spot treating, use a dishwashing solution, and attack the stains with the suds only (don't get the leather overly wet).

OPPOSITE AND LEFT
Leather or faux leather offer almost foolproof seat cushions: It's super easy to wipe up spills as soon as they happen and, in my opinion, the more wear and tear they receive, the better they look.

all-natural solutions

Though we've been schooled in the idea that we need chemical-laden products to clean a house properly, there's not a lot that distilled white vinegar can't manage—it's very acidic. I love this approach, not only because it's non-toxic to children and pets, but also because it's much friendlier to the environment and undeniably affordable.

You can attack nonporous surfaces with undiluted distilled white vinegar, but I generally add in a tiny bit of water, and some lemon, just to make it smell, well, lemony. If I need a scouring paste, I mix baking soda with a tiny bit of dishwashing detergent, and then enough vinegar to make it the right consistency.

My mother always runs vinegar through her coffeemaker to attack buildup (followed by water to eliminate any extra residue), and boils vinegar in a measuring cup in the microwave to destroy odors. I've even successfully cleaned the grime off of grout with distilled white vinegar by spraying it directly on the discoloration, letting it sit for a few minutes, and then scrubbing it with an old toothbrush.

There are a million recipes on the Internet for vinegar- and baking soda–based cleaning recipes—some combination of the two is bound to work on any nonporous surface.

To keep your all-cream or -white upholstery clean, I recommend a stainguard spray from Fiberseal, respraying every few years.

The Most Common Stains (and How to Remove Them Without Bleach)

A word of caution: Always test the solution on a hidden hem or the underside of the material first!

white rings: If water glasses leave a white mark behind on surfaces, try rubbing the stain with mayonnaise and letting it sit for an hour. Alternately, mix equal parts distilled white vinegar and vegetable oil and rub it in, going with the grain.

coffee: First, apply a mixture of soapy water (1 teaspoon of dishwashing detergent in 1 cup of water) to the stain, from the inside out (you don't want to create a water stain on top of the coffee). Follow with a mixture of vinegar and water ($1/3$ cup of vinegar, $2/3$ cup of water).

ink: Spray hair spray onto a clean towel and dab at the stain—don't rub! If that doesn't work, follow with nail polish remover or acetone (again, apply it to a clean paper or cloth towel). Finally, ensure that you've lifted all the chemicals from the fabric by finishing the process with a mild mixture of dishwashing detergent and water.

butter and oil: Use a tiny amount of solvent like Dryel, and dab into the stain, from the center out. Follow with a mixture of dishwashing detergent and water. Or sprinkle with baking soda to immediately absorb the oils.

wax: Place a paper towel over the stain and then iron the area—the heat should lift the stain right out.

red wine: First, I blot the stain (don't rub!) with white wine. You can also pour table salt on the stain to soak up as much as possible and once dry, vacuum it. If discoloration remains, I dab it with club soda, followed by a mixture of one part dishwashing detergent to two parts hydrogen peroxide.

hard water stains on metal: Fill a sandwich bag with distilled white vinegar and baking soda (2:1) and tie it to your showerhead or faucet. Let it sit for at least an hour. You can also moisten a paper towel with distilled white vinegar and wrap it around the offending metal for a few hours, before wiping it clean. If the item needs to be scrubbed, mix four parts vinegar to one part salt, and scrub.

THE ALL-WHITE BED

Putting together an all-white bed presents many challenges, from matching the various components (I solve this by sticking to one brand) to keeping white sheets white. Excessive washing will ultimately turn them grayish, an effect that can be heightened by calcium deposits from hard water. Plus, use itself is a threat. Washing your white sheets separately, at extremely high temperatures, and with a whitening detergent like OxiClean or the occasional dose of bleach is the only successful approach I've ever found.

"A lot of people worry about the 'wear and tear' on furnishings. I feel it's more a matter of people treating the things that surround them with respect."

—Albert Hadley, *The Story of America's Preeminent Interior Designer*

It's best to buy floor-kissing fabrics such as bed panels and curtains that are easily removable for biannual drycleaning. Alternatively, the now much more pleasantly textured indoor/outdoor fabrics can take a scrubbing in situ.

Decoding Thread Counts

Over the years, thread counts on sheets have climbed exponentially—it's not uncommon to find totally confounding numbers, like 1,200 or 1,400. Thread count measures the number of threads in one square inch of material (both weft and warp). But some manufacturers are trying to make their product more attractive by counting the number of strands that make up each thread and multiplying it accordingly (e.g., multiplying a thread count of 200 or 300 by four) It has become ridiculous, so try not to get taken by an expensive product whose claims of superiority are exaggerated. Also, if the threads are made up of too many parts, your sheets may fray and wear out fast, which is why they have that super-soft "sateen" effect. Bottom line, anything more than 400 is an unwarranted dramatization and anything less than 180 is too scratchy to be comfortable.

I like Egyptian cotton the best, because it's incredibly strong and cool to the touch and can suffer countless washings before it shows any wear at all. It's a complicated process, but essentially, due to an extensive carding and mercerizing process, Egyptian cotton sheets are woven from longer and stronger fibers (rather than many smaller strands rolled together). They are expensive, but they seem to last longer than other sheets.

acknowledgments

This book would not have been remotely possible were it not for the designers whose visions and labors created the rooms on these pages, and their clients, who allowed us these intimate glimpses into their homes. The designers are named in the credits but, in order to maintain privacy, the clients are not. I owe an equal debt of gratitude to the photographers and stylists who helped capture the spirit of these homes and bring us through their lenses and perspectives to see them in the most perfect light.

For me, there would have been no surviving the processes of the past year and a half (design work at Kemble Interiors, a new baby, and this book) were it not for Lindsey Herod and her supreme dedication, long hours, and general brilliance as she became my second pair of arms, legs, and eyes. Apologies are due to her husband, Clint, for her frequent hijacking. Caroline Irvin was a surprise and savior whom I didn't know how badly I would need until she jumped in and devotedly and adeptly exceeded all rational calls of duty. Buckets of gratitude to my ever-patient editor, Aliza Fogelson, not only for giving me the idea for this book, but also for being particularly gracious given my cat-on-a-leash like processes. And to Elise Loehnen, who was often left holding this leash, so I hope she enjoys laughing about it one day. Zach DeSart, my photographer-extraordinaire, thanks for putting up with me and being so good and so game.

To all of the magazines, online magazines, and bloggers who contributed, particularly: Julia Noran with the Editor at Large, *Fairfield County at Home,* British *House & Garden,* Style at Home, *Veranda, House Beautiful, Elle Décor, Traditional Home, Canadian House and Home, Architectural Digest, Connecticut Cottages and Gardens,* Condé Nast and the *House & Garden* and *Domino* archives, Lonny, Things to Inspire— what can I say . . . Without you, there wouldn't be much to look at, and your publications inspire us to live more beautiful and stylish lives. Thank you for sharing your work directly in this book and allowing me to curate and present what I have admired in your pages to illustrate the concept.

To my NYC team, who make coming to work so much fun every day: Rhea Tziros, Anna Burke, Sarah Connolly, Charlotte Barnes, Heidi Bianco, Leah Forma Nichols, Caroline Irvin, and Lindsey Herod. To our swing crew, especially: Hadley Irvine, Molly Peters, Jessica Kleinknecht, Alexandra Morris, Gail Kennedy, Danielle Armstrong, Lindsey Lane, and Jenn Grandchamp. Thanks, too, to our Palm Beach team: Franco Basurto, Marga Zurovskis, R'Lynn Allore, Patti Blank, Kerol Decristo, Leslie Gaudio, Lois Wideman, Ashley Sharpe, Lori Deeds, Keithley Miller, Kirsten Fisk, Ross Rose, Lauren Hooks, Courtney Hooks, and Brooke Hutig. And, as to thanks to my mom, Mimi McMakin, there aren't enough letters in the alphabet, or words in my vocabulary, so I just have to hope she knows.

To the team at Clarkson Potter, including: Stephanie Huntwork, Patricia Shaw, Kim Tyner, and Peggy Paul.

A huge thanks to all of the people who have lent advice and shared ideas, including my agent, Jenn Joel, Bronson Van Wyck, Lela Rose, Deborah Needleman, Dara Caponigro, Amy Vischio, Liesl Schillinger, Eddie Ross and Jaithan Kochar, Anita Sarsidi, Amanda Brooks, Kim Cutter, Jeffrey Bauman, Elana Posner, Gin Boswick, Jennifer Garland Ross, and Dylan Lauren. To my dad, Phoebe, Madeleine and Julie, and Leroy, much love, always.

To my children, Rascal, Zinnia, and now Wick, who deserve an apology but no thanks, as they did nothing but distract me from writing with hilarious antics and the magnetic pull of their general deliciousness. To my love, Boykin— if only you knew how many rolley carts it would take to carry this load, you may never have agreed to the trip. Thank you for pulling us all in the many directions you do. I know I'm a lucky girl.

Lastly, I live in absolute terror that I have neglected to credit a photographer, stylist, or designer. If I have, please e-mail me, and I will update our website, blog, and any subsequent editions of the book.

resources

CONTRACTORS AND ARTISANS

Alpha Workshops
www.alphaworkshops.org

BerryCo (graphic design)
www.annetteberrydesign.com/new

Celebrity Moving (moving and storage)
p. 718.786.1350

**Cheron Tomkins, Decorative Arts NY
(faux finishing)**
decorativeartsny.wordpress.com

Christopher Rollinson (faux finishing)
www.christopherrollinson.com

Dog Productions Inc. (custom millwork)
p. 718.782.7711

**Etched Design (antiqued mirror and
specialty surfaces)**
p. 917.207.6211

**Ilan Telmont, Spearhead LLC
(contracting)**
p. 917.304.0561

**Jaydan Interiors (upholstery and
curtains)**
www.jaydaninteriors.com

**Jaynor Delivery Inc. (moving and
delivery)**
p. 631.434.6827

**J. Edlin Interiors Ltd. (upholstery and
curtains)**
p. 212.243.2111

**Jennifer Garland Ross, Art Peritus
(antique appraisal and consulting)**
www.artperitus.com

**Jose Escobar at Design Quest Custom
(custom furniture)**
www.dqcustom.net

Miriam Ellner (eglomise)
www.miriamellner.com

**Old World Plaster—Jurgen Beneke
(custom plaster)**
www.owplaster.com

**R&A Painting and Decorating (painting
and wallpapering)**
p. 917.886.7702

**Red Star Painting (painting and
wallpapering)**
p. 917.226.2961

Well Built Company (contracting)
www.wellbuiltco.com

PAINT SOURCES

Benjamin Moore
www.benjaminmoore.com

Farrow and Ball
us.farrow-ball.com

Fine Paints of Europe
www.finepaintsofeurope.com

Pratt and Lambert
www.prattandlambert.com

Ralph Lauren
www.ralphlaurenhome.com/products/
paint

Rollinson Hues (custom paint mixing)
www.christopherrollinson.com/
rollinsonhues

Valspar Paint
www.valsparpaint.com

COLLECTIBLES AND ANTIQUES

145 Antiques
www.145antiques.com

L'Antiquaire & the Connoisseur
www.lantiquaire.us

The Antiques Garage Flea Market
www.hellskitchenfleamarket.com

Blackman & Cruz
www.blackmancruz.com

Braswell Galleries
braswellgalleries.com

Bungalow, Westport, CT
p. 203.227.4406

Duane Antiques
www.duaneantiques.com

John Rosselli
johnrosselliantiques.com

John Salibello
www.johnsalibelloantiques.com

Mondo Cane
www.mondocane.com

Sentimento Antiques
www.sentimentoantiques.com

Showplace Antique + Design Center
www.nyshowplace.com

Suzanne Golden Antiques
www.suzannegoldenantiques.com

TILE AND HARDWARE

Ann Sacks Tile & Stone
www.annsacks.com

Artistic Tile
www.artistictile.com

Complete Tile Collection
www.completetile.com

The Decorative Hardware Studio
dhshardware.com

E. R. Butler & Co
www.erbutler.com

George Taylor Specialties
p. 212.226.5369

Nanz
www.nanz.com

P. E. Guerin
www. peguerin.com

Rocky Mountain Hardware
www.rockymountainhardware.com

Sherle Wagner
www.sherlewagner.com

Simon's Hardware
www.simonsny.com

Walker Zanger
www.walkerzanger.com

Waterworks
www.waterworks.com

FABRICS, WALLCOVERS, AND TRIMS

Brunschwig & Fils
www.brunschwig.com

Clarence House
www.clarencehouse.com

Cowtan & Tout
www.cowtan.com

Farrow & Ball
www.farrow-ball.com

F. Schumacher
www.fschumacher.com

Holland & Sherry
www.hollandandsherry.com

John Rosselli & Associates
www.johnrosselliassociates.com

Kravet
www.kravet.com

Lee Jofa
www.leejofa.com

M&J Trimming
www.mjtrim.com

Madeline Weinrib
www.madelineweinrib.com

Moore & Giles
www.mooreandgilesinc.com

Osborne & Little
www.osborneandlittle.com

Phillip Jeffries Ltd. (natural texture wallcoverings)
www.phillipjeffries.com

Pindler & Pindler
www.pindler.com

Quadrille
www.quadrillefabrics.com

Ralph Lauren
www.ralphlaurenhome.com

Rogers & Goffigon
p. 212.888.3242

Samuel & Sons
www.samuelandsons.com

Scalamandré
www.scalamandre.com

Stark Fabric
www.starkfabric.com

Valtekz (faux leathers and composite fabrics)
www.valtekz.com

Zoffany
www.zoffany.com

LIGHTING

Circa Lighting
www.circalighting.com

Currey & Company
www.curreycodealers.com

Frederick Cooper
www.frederickcooper.com

Robert Abbey, Inc.
www.robertabbey.com

Solaria
www.solaria.com

RUGS

Beauvais
www.beauvaiscarpets.com

Doris Leslie Blau
www.dorisleslieblau.com

Galerie Shabab
www.galerieshabab.com

JD Staron
www.jdstaron.com

Kyle Bunting
www.kylebunting.com

Merida Meridian
www.meridameridian.com

Patterson, Flynn & Martin
www.pattersonflynnmartin.com

Rosemary Hallgarten
www.rosemaryhallgarten.com

Rosenfeld Carpet
www.rosenfeldcarpet.com

Stark
www.starkcarpets.com

ENTERTAINING, ACCESSORIES, AND DETAILS

Abat-Jour (custom lampshades)
p. 212.753.5455

Accessory Store LLC, Stamford, CT
stamfordshades.com

Creative Candles
www.creativecandles.com

Diane James Home (artificial floral arrangements)
www.dianejameshome.com

D. Porthault
www.dporthaultparis.com

Dransfield & Ross (tabletop and accessories)
www.dransfieldandross.biz

far4
far4.net/shop

The Future Perfect
www.thefutureperfect.com

Jardins en Fleur
www.jardinsenfleur.com

Jayson Home & Garden
www.jaysonhomeandgarden.com

John Derian
www.johnderian.com

John Robshaw (bedding and accessories)
www.johnrobshaw.com

Jonathan Adler
www.jonathanadler.com

Julia B. (bedding and linens)
www.juliab.com

Leron Linens
www.leron.com

Muji
www.muji.us

mydeco
us.mydeco.com

Pratesi Luxury Home Linens
www.pratesi.com

Rani Aribela
www.raniarabella.com

Shades of the Midnight Sun, Bronxville, NY
p. 914.779.7237

Shandell's, Millerton, NY (custom lampshades)
www. shandells.com

Sharyn Blond Linens
www.sharynblondlinens.com

Sweet Lisa's Exquisite Cakes, Greenwich, CT (cupcakes)
www.sweetlisas.com

Tessera Collection
www.tesseracollection.com

Time Frame
www.timeframeonline.com

Treillage
www.bunnywilliams.com/treillage

Waylande Gregory Studios
waylandegregory.com

FURNITURE

A + R Store
www.aplusrstore.com

Aidan Gray
www.aidangrayhome.com

Anthropologie
www.anthropologie.com

Ballard Designs
www.ballarddesigns.com

Blackman Cruz
www.blackmancruz.com

Calypso St. Barth
www.calypsostbarth.com

Canal Plastics
p. 212.925.1032

CB2
www.cb2.com

Ceylon Portfolio
dirtyfuture.com/ceylonetcie/ceylon-portfolio

Crate and Barrel
www.crateandbarrel.com

Design Within Reach
www.dwr.com

Desiron
www.desiron.com

Duc Duc
www.ducducnyc.com

The Future Perfect
www.thefutureperfect.com

Generate Design
www.gnr8.biz

Ikea
www.ikea.com

Jerry Pair
www.jerrypair.com

Kemble Interiors Inc., Palm Beach
www.kembleinteriors.com

Laneventure
www.laneventure.com

Lee Industries
www.leeindustries.com

Mecox Gardens
www.mecoxgardens.com

Mitchell Gold + Bob Williams
www.mgandbw.com

MoMA Store
www.momastore.org

Moss
www.mossonline.com

Nessen Showroom
www.nessenshowroom.com

Noir
www.noirfurniturela.com

Odegard
www.odegardinc.com

Oly Studio
www.olystudio.com

Plexi-Craft
www.plexi-craft.com

Ralph Lauren Furniture
www.ralphlaurenhome.com/products/
furniture

Restoration Hardware
www.restorationhardware.com

Room & Board
www.roomandboard.com

Tritter Feefer
www.tritterfeefer.com

Unica Home
www.unicahome.com

Velocity Art & Design
velocityartanddesign.com

Venfield
www.venfieldnyc.com

West Elm
www.westelm.com

ART CONSULTANTS,
GALLERIES, AND FRAMERS

Blair Clarke of Voltz Clarke LLC
www.voltzclarke.com

David Findlay Jr. Gallery
www.davidfindlayjr.com

Elizabeth Sadoff & Associates (art
consultant)
esadoff.com

J. Pocker (framing)
www.jpocker.com

Kipton Art
www.kiptonart.com

Steven Amedee (framing)
www.stevenamedee.com

Wally Findlay
www.wallyfindlay.com

ONE-OF-A-KIND AND
AUCTIONS

1st Dibs
www.1stdibs.com

Bonanza
www.bonanza.com

Bonhams
www.bonhams.com

Christie's
www.christies.com

Doyle
www.doylenewyork.com

eBay
www.ebay.com

Etsy
www.etsy.com

RENDERERS

John Gibson
www.johngibson-perspectives.com

Rick High
p. 561.655.1859

CLEANING

Caldrea
www.caldrea.com

Fiberseal
www.fiberseal.com

The Laundress
thelaundress.com

Maas Silver Polish
www.maasinc.com

Manhattan Wardrobe Supply (all things
cleaning)
www.wardrobesupply.com

Mr. Clean Magic Eraser
www.mrclean.com

Mrs. Meyers
www.mrsmeyers.com

photograph credits

Photographs on pages 74 and 108 (below right) courtesy of *Elle Décor,* copyright by William Abranowicz / Art + Commerce.

Photograph on page 156 (below left) copyright by Caroline Arber / moodboard / Corbis.

Photographs on pages 31 (above left) and 176 (right) courtesy of Fairfield County at Home; on pages 182–183 and 214–215 copyright by Stacy Bass.

Photograph on page 120 courtesy of British *House & Garden,* copyright by Bill Batten.

Photograph on page 206 copyright by Steve Baxter / Digital Vision / Getty Images.

Photograph on page 137 courtesy of *Architectural Digest,* copyright by Gordon Beall.

Photograph on page 87 (bottom right) copyright by Eric Bean / Photographer's Choice / Getty Images.

Photograph on page 186 copyright by the estate of Fernando Bengoechea.

Photograph on page 87 (bottom center) copyright by Hans Berggren / Johner Images / Getty Images.

Photograph on page 106 courtesy of *Traditional Home* / Meredith Corp.; on page 124 courtesy of *Traditional Home* / Meredith Corp., copyright by John Bessler.

Photograph on page 192 courtesy of Bonhams.

Photographs on pages 193 and 198 courtesy of *House Beautiful,* copyright Antoine Bootz.

Photograph on page 54 courtesy of *Elle Décor,* copyright by Henry Bourne.

Photograph on page 180 (top left) copyright by Charles Brooks.

Photograph on page 242 (bottom) copyright by Lauren Burke / Lifesize / Getty Images.

Photograph on page 98 (above left) copyright by Eric Cahan.

Photograph on page 167 copyright by Carai.

Photograph on page 87 (top right) copyright by CP Cheah / Flickr / Getty Images.

Photographs on pages 19 (above left), 28 (center), 29 (above), 58, 80 (center), 92 (top), 96 (below left), 105 (top right), 108 (top), 109 (below left), 110 (bottom), 145 (bottom), 152, 158 (bottom), 175 (below right), 203 (left), 216–217, 219 (middle left), 220 (center, bottom left, bottom right), 222 (left), all courtesy of *Lonny Magazine,* copyright by Patrick Cline.

Photographs on pages 12–13, 28–29 (bottom), 50, 52, 78, 80 (left and right), 127 (top), 142 (below left), 156 (above left) copyright by Willie Cole Photography.

Photographs on pages 72 (bottom) and 228 (top left) copyright by Grey Crawford.

Photograph on page 189 (right) copyright by Mark Cutler.

Photographs on pages 2, 6, 8–9, 11, 31 (above right), 42 (bottom), 46, 49, 51 (left), 60 (left), 64, 66–67, 73, 76 (right), 77, 79, 81, 82, 83, 84–85, 91, 99, 100, 101 (above left), 112–113, 121 (top), 126, 127 (below right), 134 (above left), 136 (right), 141, 142 (top left), 150, 151, 155, 157, 160, 161, 166 (top right and bottom right), 171, 173, 196–197, 205, 207, 208 (top right), 209, 211 (top left, bottom center, bottom right), 218, 219 (top center), 220 (top left and top right), 225 (bottom), 226, 229, 232 (bottom), 233, 237, 246 copyright by Zach DeSart.

Photographs on pages 16–17, 224–225, 234, 235 (left and right) copyright by Adrien Dirand.

Photographs on pages 26–27 and 117 (below right) copyright by Sarah Dorio.

Photographs on pages 170 (left), 180 (right), 184 (top), 221, 223 copyright by Christopher Drake.

Photograph on page 87 (top left) copyright by Michael Duva / Stone+ / Getty Images.

Photographs on pages 5, 20 (above right), 36 (right), 37 (left), 56, 57, 70, 72 (top), 76 (left), 101 (bottom), 117 (top right), 178 (bottom), 199, 208 (left), 210, 219 (bottom right), 228 (bottom), 235 (center), 240 (top) courtesy of *Elle Décor;* pages 240 (bottom) and 241 copyright by Pieter Estersohn.

Photograph on page 159 (bottom) copyright by EWA / Arcaid 2011.

Photograph on page 87 (bottom left) copyright by Don Farrall / Photodisc / Getty Images.

Photograph on page 164 (bottom) courtesy of *Architectural Digest,* copyright by Marina Faust.

Photograph on page 118 copyright by Ferm Living.

Photographs on pages 97 and 190 copyright by Miguel Flores Vianna / The Editor at Large / TIA Digital Ltd.

Photograph on pages 230–231 courtesy of *House Beautiful,* copyright by Scott Francis.

Photographs on pages 22, 62, 69 (left), 75 (right), 88, 94 (left), 104, 107, 108 (bottom left), 127 (below left), 128–129, 131 (top), 145 (top), 154 (left), 164 (top left and right), 168–169, 172 (right), 188, 203 (right), 204 (bottom left), 211 (bottom left) copyright by Douglas Friedman.

Photographs on pages 116 (right), 148 (top left), 222 (right) copyright by Nicole Hill Gerulat.

Photographs on pages 219 (bottom left) and 239 copyright by Grant K. Gibson.

Photograph on page 149 copyright by Josh Gibson.

Photographs on pages 132 (right) and 184 (bottom) courtesy of *House Beautiful,* copyright by Oberto Gili.

Photographs on pages 63, 156 (above right), 204 (top left), 212–213 copyright by Tria Giovan.

Photographs on pages 30, 105 (center right), 121 (bottom), 122, 123, 133, 144, 175 (top left and right), 177, 216, 219 (middle center), 228 (top right) from the archives of Canadian *House & Home,* copyright by Michael Graydon.

Photograph on page 219 (center right) copyright by Ken Gutmaker.

Photographs on pages 14 and 116 (left) copyright by Francois Halard / trunkarchive .com.

designer and architect credits

Traci Alleman
Page 185 (top)

James Aman of Aman & Carson Interiors
www.amancarson.com
Page 36 (right)

James Aman & Anne Carson of Aman & Carson Interiors
www.amancarson.com
Pages 230–231

Jeff Andrews Designs
www.jeffandrews-design.com
Page 19 (top right)

Michael Angus
Page 30

Eldridge Arnold
www.eldridgearnold.com
Page 172 (top left)

Felix Flit and Marina Lanina
www.autuncontractors.com
Pages 12–13, 28–29 (bottom), 50 (right), 52, 127 (top)

Ash Suri
www.autuncontractors.com
Page 50 (left)

Kimberly Ayres
www.kimberlyayres.com
Page 98 (left)

Michael Bargo
www.michaelbargo.com
Pages 128–129, 154 (left), 203 (right)

Stéphane Beel Architecten
www.stephanebeel.com
Page 96 (top left)

Jeffrey Bilhuber
www.bilhuber.com
Page 20 (bottom)

Meg Braff
www.megbraff.com
Page 149

Keith Brown
Pages 26–27 and 117 (bottom right)

Nannette Brown
Pages 191 and 202

Burnham Design
www.burnhamdesign.com
Pages 72 (bottom) and 228 (top left)

Libby Cameron
www.libbycameron.com
Pages 89 (top) and 186

Jesse Carrier, Carrier & Co.
www.carrierandcompany.com
Pages 100, 126, 141, 142 (top left), 160 (top left)

Dara Caponigro
Pages 41 (bottom), 47, 89 (bottom)

Laurann Claridge
Pages 145 (bottom), 203 (left), 220 (bottom right)

Leslie Cohen
www.lesliecohendesign.com
Pages 109 (top right) and 143

Wende Cohen for Bungalow, Westport, CT
p. 203.227.4406
Pages 214–215

Eric Cohler
www.ericcohler.com
Page 165

Jennifer Coleman, JKC Design
www.jkcinteriordesigns.com
Page 117 (left)

Gul Coskun
www.coskunfineart.com
Page 243

Cullman & Kravis
www.cullmankravis.com
Page 134 (bottom left)

Mark Cutler
www.markcutlerdesign.com
Page 189 (right)

Laura Day
www.lauradayliving.com
Pages 36 (top left), 65, 101 (top right)

Sarah Delaney and Michaelis Boyd Associates
www.sarahdelaneydesign.co.uk
www.michaelisboyd.com
Page 96 (center left)

John Derian
www.johnderian.com
Page 204 (top right)

Joseph Dirand
www.josephdirand.com
Pages 16–17, 224–225, 234, 235 (left and right)

John Dransfield & Geoffrey Ross
www.dransfieldandross.biz
Pages 60–61, 98 (top right), 136 (left)

Nathan Egan Interiors
www.nathanegan.com
Page 48

Ethan Feirstein & Ari Heckman
www.ashnyc.com
Page 19 (top left)

Waldo Fernandez
www.waldosdesigns.com
Pages 32–33

Brad Ford
www.bradfordid.com
Pages 40, 58, 90 (top, center, bottom), 106, 124, 124–125, 181

Barbara Franceski
www.barbarafranceski.com
Page 69 (right)

Barclay Fryery
p. 203.862.9662
Pages 59 and 194–195

Anthony Gianacakos
Page 29 (top)

Grant K. Gibson
www.grantkgibson.com
Pages 219 (bottom left) and 239

Philip Gorrivan
www.philipgorrivan.com
Pages 133, 162, 163 (top left)

Allan Greenberg Architect
www.allangreenberg.com
Page 134 (bottom left)

Carol Groh and Associates
Page 37 (right)

Victoria Hagan
www.victoriahagan.com
Page 19 (bottom)

Mark Hampton
www.markhampton.com
Page 21

Wendy Harrop & Olivia Gregory
Page 120

Haus Interior
www.hausinterior.com
Page 175 (bottom right)

Katherine Hodge, Sage Design
www.sagedesign.com
Page 142 (bottom left)

William Hodgins
Pages 184 (bottom), 193, 198

Philip Hooper & Sally Metcalfe
Page 93 (top)

Eric Hughes
Page 204 (bottom right)

Gary Hutton
www.garyhuttondesign.com
Pages 34, 38, 135, 148 (bottom left, bottom right, and top right)

Lisa Jackson and Lucca & Co.
Pages 92 (bottom), 94 (top right), 102 (right), 219 (top left and bottom right), 228 (bottom), 232 (top)

Jay Jeffers
www.jeffersdesigngroup.com
Page 166 (bottom left)

Donna Karan
www.donnakaranhome.com
Pages 88 and 104

Carole Katleman & Daniel Cuevas
Pages 18 (left) and 201

Kelley Interior Design
www.kelleyinteriordesign.com
Pages 53 and 163 (top right)

Kemble Interiors, Inc.
www.kembleinteriors.com
Pages 6, 8–9, 11, 12–13, 28–29 (bottom), 31 (right), 49, 50 (right), 51 (left), 52, 60 (left), 64 (top and bottom), 66–67, 73, 76 (right), 77, 78, 79, 80, 81, 82, 83, 84–85, 91, 99, 108 (top), 110 (bottom), 112–113, 121 (top), 127, 150, 151, 155, 156 (top left), 157, 158 (bottom), 160 (bottom), 161, 209, 211 (top left), 216–217, 218, 220 (top left, top right, center, and bottom left), 225 (bottom), 226, 229, 232 (bottom), 233, 237, 246

Pat King
Page 204 (top left)

Rita Konig
Pages 42 (bottom), 173, 205 (top)

Richard Keith Langham, Inc.
www.richardkeithlangham.com
Pages 5 and 70

Stephen Knollenberg
www.stephenknollenberg.com
Page 137

Jackye Lanham
www.jackyelanham.com
Pages 212–213

Amy Lau
www.amylaudesign.com
Pages 42 (top) and 156 (bottom right)

Michael Leva
Pages 57 and 117 (top right)

Robert K Lewis
Page 179 (bottom)

Roger Lussier
Pages 24–25

J.Crew/Jenna Lyons
Page 219 (middle left)

Ned Marshall and Henry Norton
Page 132 (top right)

Ron Marvin
www.ronmarvin.com
Page 28 (center)

Mary McDonald
www.marymcdonaldinc.com
Pages 18 (right) and 23

Marian McEvoy
Page 179 (top)

James McIntyre
Pages 121 (bottom) and 122

San Ming
Page 153

Shelley Morris Interior Design Ltd.
www.shelleymorrisinteriors.com
Pages 31 (left) and 176 (right)

Tracy Morris
www.tracymorrisdesign.com
Page 102 (left)

Christina Murphy
www.christinamurphyinteriors.com/
Page 222 (left)

Deborah Needleman
Page 105 (top right)

Michelle Nussbaumer
www.ceylonetcie.com
Pages 44–45, 101 (bottom), 138–139

Thomas O'Brien
Page 41 (bottom)

ODADA
Odada.net
Pages 146–147

Ellen O'Neill
Page 210

Jill O'Shea
Pages 182–183

Pamplemousse Design
www.pamplemoussedesign.com
Pages 14, 74, 108 (bottom right), 167

Gail Plechaty of Real Simple Design
p. 847.356.1111
Pages 28 (top), 75 (left), 244–245

Popham Design
www.pophamdesign.com
Pages 114 and 134 (right)

Jennifer Post
www.jenniferpostdesign.com
Page 43